KB075621

가상현실 게임 개발

가상현실 게임 개발

발　행 | 2022년 10월 31일
저　자 | 류 석원
펴낸이 | 한건희
펴낸곳 | 주식회사 부크크
출판사등록 | 2014.07.15.(제2014-16호)
주　소 | 서울특별시 금천구 가산디지털1로 119 SK트윈타워 A동 305호
전　화 | 1670-8316
이메일 | info@bookk.co.kr

ISBN | 979-11-372-9957-3

www.bookk.co.kr

가상현실 게임 개발

류 석원 지음

CONTENT

오늘날 4차 산업과 메타버스는 가장 중요한 분야가 되었으며, 이를 구현하기 위해서 게임 엔진을 사용한다. 이 책에서는 현재 많이 사용하고 있는 unity 게임 엔진에 대해 기초부터 하나하나 설명하면서, 초보자들도 이해할 수 있는 간단하고 단순한 게임을 만들어 본다.

Unity 게임 엔진에 대한 기초 지식을 익히고, 3차원 형태의 게임 제작 방법에 대해 알아본다. C# 프로그램 언어를 사용하여 게임 제작에 필요한 스크립트를 작성하는 방법에 대해 공부하고, scene에다 객체를 추가하는 방법과 스크립트를 통해 객체의 기능을 구현하는 방법에 대해서도 공부한다.

이 책이 3차원 게임 분야에 관심을 가지고 있는 분들에게 도움이 되기를 바란다.

柳 碩垣

Chapter 1. Foundation

Unity 3D Game Engine은 Unreal Game Engine과 함께 게임 제작 시 제일 많이 사용하는 게임 엔진이다. 사용하기 편하고 실행이 바로 진행되므로 결과를 빠르게 볼 수 있는 장점이 있다.

1. Unity 다운로드하고 설치하는 법

https://unity3d.com/kr 방문한다 〉 지금 Unity 다운로드 click 〉 Personal Edition 아래에 있는 무료 다운로드 click 〉 플랫폼에서 Window 선택하고 설치프로그램 다운로드 click 〉 실행 button click한다.

2. Unity 실행하고 새 프로젝트 만드는 법

Unity icon double click 〉 Project 화면에서 New 선택 〉 Project name = U_3D_BallGame 〉 3D 2D에서 3D 선택 〉 Create Project button click 〉 잠시 기다린다.

Project 저장위치는 C:\ Users 〉 USER 〉 Documents 〉 아래에 저장된다. C:\ User 〉 Public 〉 Documents 〉 Unity Projects 〉 Unity Version 2017.3.1. 〉 아래에 내가 만든 프로젝트 이름으로 저장한다.

3. 새로 만든 project의 Unity Scene을 저장하는 법

메뉴 File 〉 Save Scene 선택한다. 저장되는 위치는 내 PC \ C:\ 사용자 (= Users) 〉 공용(= User) 〉 공용 문서 (= Documents) 〉 Unity Projects 〉 U_3D_BallGame (= Project name) 〉 Assets 〉 아래에 저장

된다.

Unity 3D Editor를 보면 가운데에 있는 3D 공간은 게임 영역을 디자인하는 공간이고, 왼쪽 위에 있는 Hierarchy는 게임에 사용되는 구성요소 (= Actor) 들을 보여주고, 왼쪽 아래에 있는 Project는 게임 실행에 필요한 material, script, model들을 보여주고, 오른쪽에 있는 Inspector는 게임 속의 구성요소들의 특성들을 보여준다.

4. Plane을 사용하여 바닥을 만드는 법

메뉴 Game Object 〉 3D Object 〉 Plane click 〉 Plane 추가된다 〉 왼쪽 Hierarchy에서 Plane을 천천히 두 번 선택 〉 이름을 Ground라고 수정한다 〉 오른쪽 Inspector에서 〉 Transform rollout 〉 오른쪽 톱니바퀴 click 〉 Reset click 〉 초기값으로 설정된다 〉 그 아래에서 0, 0, 0, 0, 0, 0,   1.2, 1, 1.2 로 수정한다.

5. 선택한 Game Object 중심으로 보는 법

왼쪽 Hierarchy에서 중심으로 보고 싶은 Game Object 선택 〉 메뉴 Edit 〉 Lock View to Selected 선택한다 〉 그러면 선택한 game object 중심으로 전체가 보이도록 camera가 이동한다.

가운데 버튼을 누르고 마우스를 이동하면, 손바닥으로 화면을 미는 효과이고 (카메라 이동효과), 가운데 버튼을 위로 올리면 확대되고, 아래로 내리면 축소된다. 오른쪽 버튼 누르고 마우스를 이동하면, 카메라 회전 효과이다. 왼쪽 버튼 누르면 object가 선택된다.

6. Sphere를 사용하여 공을 만드는 법

메뉴 Game Object 〉 3D Object 〉 Sphere 선택 〉 Sphere 추가된다 〉 왼쪽 Hierarchy에서 Sphere를 천천히 두 번 선택 〉 이름을 Player라고 수정한다 〉 오른쪽 Inspector에서 〉 Transform rollout 〉 오른쪽 끝 톱니바퀴 click 〉 Reset click 〉 초기값으로 설정된다 〉 그 아래에서 4, 0.5, -2,   0, 0, 0,   1, 1, 1 로 수정한다.

7. Game Object에 material을 입히는 방법 (기본 색상을 변경하는 법)

왼쪽 아래 Project 아래에서 〉 Assets folder 선택하고 〉 RMB click 〉 Create 〉 Folder 선택 〉 새 folder 추가된다 〉 이름을 Materials 로 수정한다 〉 새로 만들어진 Materials folder 선택 〉 Project 아래에 있는 Create 버튼 click 〉 Material 선택한다 〉 그러면 Materials folder 아래에 New Material 추가된다 〉 이름을 BackGround로 수정한다 〉 해당 material을 선택한다 〉 오른쪽 Inspector에서 〉 Main Maps 아래에 있는 Albedo 옆의 하얀색 색상을 click 〉 RGBA = 0, 50, 100, 255 선택 〉 파란색이 만들어진다.

왼쪽 아래 Project 아래에서 〉 Assets folder 〉 Materials folder 〉 BackGround material을 click & drag 형태로 바닥인 Plane 위에 가져다 놓는다 〉 그러면 바닥에 선택한 파란색 material이 입혀지게 된다.

8. 태양 역할을 하는 Directional Light 위치를 변경하는 법

왼쪽 Hierarchy에서 Directional Light 선택 〉 오른쪽 Inspector 〉 Transform rollout 〉 그 아래에서 0, 3, 0,   50, 60, 0,   1, 1, 1 로 수정한다.

9. Player인 공을 움직이기 위해서 Rigid Body component를 추가하는 법

왼쪽 Hierarchy에서 Player 선택 〉 공이 선택된다 〉 오른쪽 Inspector에서 맨 아래에 있는 Add Component click 〉 Physics 〉 Rigid Body 선택 〉 그러면 Inspector에 Rigid Body component가 추가된다.

참고로, Unity에서 game object를 움직이게 하려면 Rigid body component를 추가해야 한다. 구체적으로 움직이는 프로그램은 visual studio 2015 script로 작성한다.

10. Player인 공을 움직이기 위한 script 작성법

왼쪽 아래 Project 아래에서 〉 Assets folder 선택하고 〉 RMB click 〉 Create 〉 Folder 선택 〉 새 folder 추가된다 〉 이름을 Scripts 로 수정한다.

왼쪽 Hierarchy에서 Player 선택 〉 오른쪽 Inspector에서 맨 아래에 있는 Add Component 버튼 click 〉 맨 아래 New Script 선택 〉 Name = PlayerController로 쓴다 〉 Language는 C# 선택 〉 Create and Add button click한다 〉 그러면 왼쪽 아래 Project 〉 Assets folder 아래에 C# 이라고 쓰인 PlayerController가 추가된다 〉 이것을 집어다가 Click&Drag 형태로 Scripts folder 안으로 이동시킨다.

Script를 작성하기 위해서, Project 〉 Assets folder 〉 Scripts folder 〉 PlayerController를 double click 〉 그러면 Visual Studio가 실행된다 〉 아래 script를 작성한다.

〈Script #1〉

```
using UnityEngine;
using System.Collections;
using System.Collections.Generic;

public class PlayerController : MonoBehaviour {
    public float speed = 10.0f;      //1  moving speed of ball
    private Rigidbody rb;            //1  ball itself
    private float MoveHorizontal;
                                  //1  horizontal movement of ball
    private float MoveVertical;    //1  vertical movement of ball
    private Vector3 movement;       //1  final movement of ball

    // Use this for initialization
    void Start () {
        rb = GetComponent<Rigidbody>();  //1  ball itself
    }

    // Update is called once per frame
    void FixedUpdate () {
                            //1  FixedUpdate() instead of Update()

        // Get key inputs to make ball roll around
        MoveHorizontal = Input.GetAxis("Horizontal");
                            //1  horizontal movement of ball
```

```
        MoveVertical = Input.GetAxis("Vertical");
                                //1  vertical movement of ball

        movement = new Vector3(MoveHorizontal, 0.0f,
                        MoveVertical);  //1  final movement of ball
        rb.AddForce(movement * speed);
                        //1  modify direction of ball movement
    }
}
```

Script 작성 후에, 메뉴 Build 〉 Solution Build 선택 〉 compile 한다 〉 아래를 보면 Error list tab과 Output tab이 있는데 Output tab에서 Build: 1 Succeeded 0 failed 메시지가 나오면 제대로 compile 된 것이다 〉 메뉴 File 〉 모두 저장 선택해서 저장한다 〉 Visual Studio를 종료한다 〉 Unity Editor로 온다.

왼쪽 Hierarchy에서 Player 선택 〉 오른쪽 Inspector 〉 Player Controller (Script) 아래를 보면 Speed = 10으로 되어 있다 〉 그 이유는 script 작성에서 speed 변수가 public 형태이기 때문이다. 즉, public float speed = 10.0f 때문이다. 앞으로는 script 자체를 수정할 필요 없이 여기서 speed 값을 수정하면 된다.

지금까지 만든 내용을 가지고 실제 게임을 실행하기 위해서 가운데에 있는 화면 위에 있는 Game tab click 〉 카메라에서 바라보는 Game mode로 바뀐다 〉 위에 있는 삼각형 Play button click 〉 게임이 실행된다 〉

ADWS 키를 누르면 공이 왼쪽, 오른쪽, 뒤쪽, 앞쪽으로 이동한다.

게임 실행 중에 일시 정지시키려면 가운데에 있는 Pause button click 한다. 게임을 재실행하려면 Pause button을 다시 누른다. 게임 실행을 완전히 정지 시키려면 삼각형 Play button을 다시 click 한다. 다시 Design mode로 되돌아가려면 Scene tab을 click 한다.

11. Camera가 Player인 공을 따라오게 하는 법

Hierarchy에서 Main Camera 선택 〉 디자인 화면인 Scene 화면 아래 오른쪽에 카메라에서 보이는 장면이 나타난다 〉 Inspector에서 〉 Transform rollout 〉 아래 값들을 4, 10, -10, 45, 0, 0, 1, 1, 1 로 수정한다 〉 그러면 camera가 위에서 45도 각도로 내려다보게 된다.

왼쪽 Hierarchy에서 Main Camera 선택 〉 오른쪽 Inspector에서 아래에 있는 Add Component 버튼 click 〉 맨 아래 New Scripts 선택 〉 Name = CameraController 로 쓴다 〉 C# 선택 〉 Create and Add button click한다 〉 그러면 왼쪽 아래 Project 〉 Assets folder 아래에 CameraController 추가된다 〉 이것을 집어다가 Scripts folder 안으로 이동시킨다.

Script를 작성하기 위해서, Project 〉 Assets folder 〉 Scripts folder 〉 CameraController를 double click 〉 그러면 Visual Studio가 실행된다 〉 아래 script를 작성한다.

〈Script #2〉

```
using UnityEngine;
using System.Collections;
using System.Collections.Generic;

public class CameraController : MonoBehaviour {
    public GameObject Player;  //2  ball
    private Vector3 offset;
            //2  distance from camera to the ball (= Player)

    // Use this for initialization
    void Start () {
        offset = transform.position - Player.transform.position;
            //2  distance from camera to the ball (= Player)
    }

    // Update is called once per frame
    void FixedUpdate ()  //2  FixedUpdate() instead of Update()
    {
        transform.position = Player.transform.position + offset;
            //2  update position of camera at every frame
    }
}
```

Script 작성 후에, 메뉴 Build 〉 솔루션 빌드 선택해서 컴파일하고 〉 메뉴 File 〉 모두 저장 선택해서 저장한다 〉 Visual Studio를 종료한다 〉

Unity Editor로 온다.

왼쪽 Hierarchy에서 Main Camera 선택 〉 오른쪽 Inspector 〉 Camera Controller (Script) 아래를 보면 Player 옆이 None (GameObject)로 되어 있다 〉 왼쪽 Hierarchy에서 Player를 click & drag 형태로 끌어다가 이 빈칸에 넣는다.

메뉴 File 〉 Save Scene 선택해서 저장한다 〉 가운데 디자인 화면에서 Game tab 선택 〉 게임을 play 해보면 키값에 따라 공이 이동하는데 카메라가 일정한 거리를 두고 따라간다. 그런데 회전은 안하고 이동만 해서 제대로 보인다.

참고로, player가 사람인 경우 일반적인 3인칭 camera를 만들려면, Hierarchy에서 camera가 player의 child가 되도록 camera를 끌어다가 player 아래에 넣으면 된다. 그러나 이 예제에서는 player가 사람이 아닌 공이므로 이와 같은 방식으로 camera를 sphere 아래에 넣어서 child로 만들면 sphere의 회전축이 3개가 되어 회전할 때 camera도 따라서 회전하는 문제가 생긴다.

12. Cylinder를 사용하여 4개의 wall을 만드는 법

벽이 4개가 이므로 이것들을 담을 Walls라는 이름의 빈 folder를 하나 만들기 위해서, 메뉴 Game Object 〉 Create Empty 선택 〉 Hierarchy에 Game Object 추가된다 〉 추가된 Game Object의 이름을 Walls로 수정한다 〉 Walls 선택 〉 오른쪽 Inspector 〉 Transform rollout 〉 오른쪽 톱니바퀴 click 〉 Reset 선택한다 〉 그러면 아래 숫자들이 초기화 된다. 참

고로, 앞으로 만들어질 벽 4개는 Walls folder의 위치에서 상대적으로 만들어지므로 Walls folder의 위치를 reset 시키는 것은 매우 중요한 일이다.

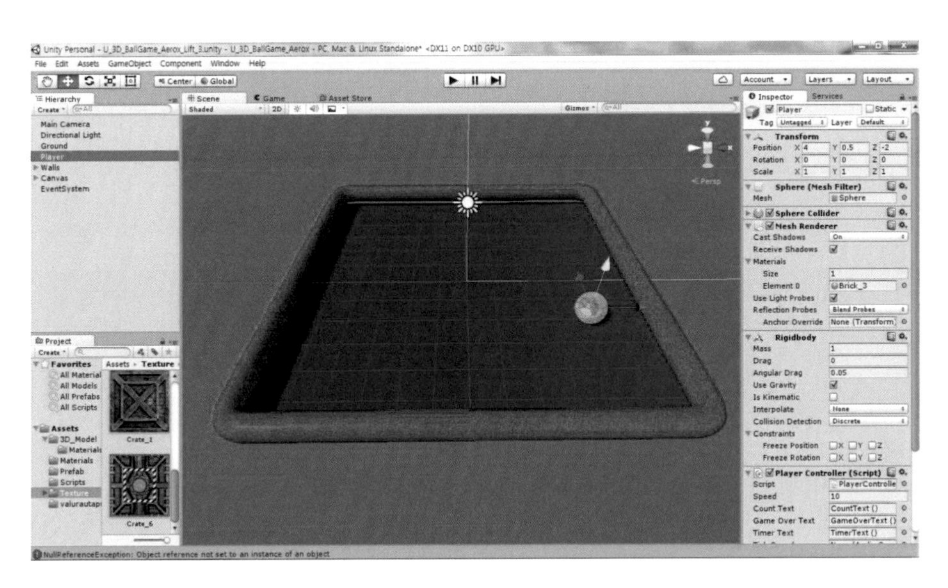

Fig 1. Ground, wall, and player

벽으로 사용할 Cylinder를 추가하기 위해서, 메뉴 Game Object 〉 3D Object 〉 Cylinder 선택 〉 Hierarchy에서 Cylinder를 집어다가 Walls folder 아래로 넣는다 〉 이름을 WallLeft로 수정한다 〉 오른쪽 Inspector 〉 Transform rollout 〉 아래의 숫자들을 -6, 0.5, 0, 90, 0, 0, 1, 6, 1로 수정한다.

왼쪽 Hierarchy 〉 Walls 아래에 있는 WallLeft 선택 〉 메뉴 Edit 〉 Copy와 Paste 명령어를 사용하여 아래와 같이 벽을 추가한다.

WallRight 만들고 6, 0.5, 0, 90, 0, 0, 1, 6, 1로 수정한다 〉

WallTop 만들고 0, 0.5, 6, 90, 90, 0, 1, 6, 1로 수정한다 〉

WallBottom 만들고 0, 0.5, -6, 90, 90, 0, 1, 6, 1로 수정한다 〉

바닥에 파란색을 입힌 것처럼 벽에도 빨간색을 입힌다 〉 메뉴 File 〉 Save Scene 선택해서 저장한다.

13. Cube를 사용하여 회전하는 pickup object를 만드는 법
메뉴 Game Object 〉 3D Object 〉 Cube 선택 〉 Cube가 추가된다 〉 Hierarchy에서 이름을 PickUp으로 수정한다 〉 오른쪽 Inspector 〉 Transform rollout 〉 아래 숫자를 0, 0.5, -5, 45, 45, 45, 0.5, 0.5, 0.5 로 수정한다.

왼쪽 Hierarchy에서 PickUp 선택 〉 오른쪽 Inspector에서 아래에 있는 Add Component 버튼 click 〉 맨 아래 New Scripts 선택 〉 Name = Rotator 로 쓴다 〉 C# 선택 〉 Create and Add button click한다 〉 그러면 왼쪽 아래 Project 〉 Assets folder 아래에 Rotator 추가된다 〉 이것을 집어다가 Scripts folder 안으로 이동시킨다.

Script를 작성하기 위해서, Project 〉 Assets folder 〉 Scripts folder 〉 Rotator를 double click 〉 그러면 Visual Studio가 실행된다 〉 아래 script를 작성한다.

〈Script #3〉

```
using UnityEngine;
using System.Collections;
using System.Collections.Generic;
```

```
public class Rotator : MonoBehaviour {
    // Use this for initialization
    void Start () {
    }

    // Update is called once per frame
    void FixedUpdate () {  //3 FixedUpdate() instead of Update()
        transform.Rotate(new Vector3(15, 30, 45) *
            Time.deltaTime);
            //3  update rotation of PickUp item at every frame
    }
}
```

Script 작성 후에, Compile 하고나서 저장한다 〉 Visual Studio를 종료한다 〉 Unity Editor로 온다.

14. PickUp game object에 실제 texture material을 입히는 방법
왼쪽 아래 Project 아래에서 〉 Assets folder 선택하고 〉 RMB click 〉 Create 〉 Folder 선택 〉 새 folder 추가된다 〉 이름을 Texture로 수정한다.

왼쪽 Project 〉 Assets 선택하고 〉 메뉴 Assets 〉 Import New Asset 〉 256x256 texture Crate_1.jpg import한다 〉 이것을 click & drag 형태로 끌어다가 Project 〉 Assets 〉 Texture로 이동시킨다 〉 Texture folder 아래에 있는 Crate_1.jpg를 click & drag 형태로 끌어다가 Scene에 보이

는 PickUp game object에 바로 입힌다.

참고로, Project 〉 Assets 〉 Texture 아래에 Materials folder가 있는데 이것은 현재 사용하고 있는 texture를 의미한다. 이것을 가져다가 game object에 입혀도 된다. 그런데, 한번이라도 사용한 texture이어야 material이 생성된다. Texture로 import했어도 사용하지 않으면 Material folder에는 생성되지 않는다.

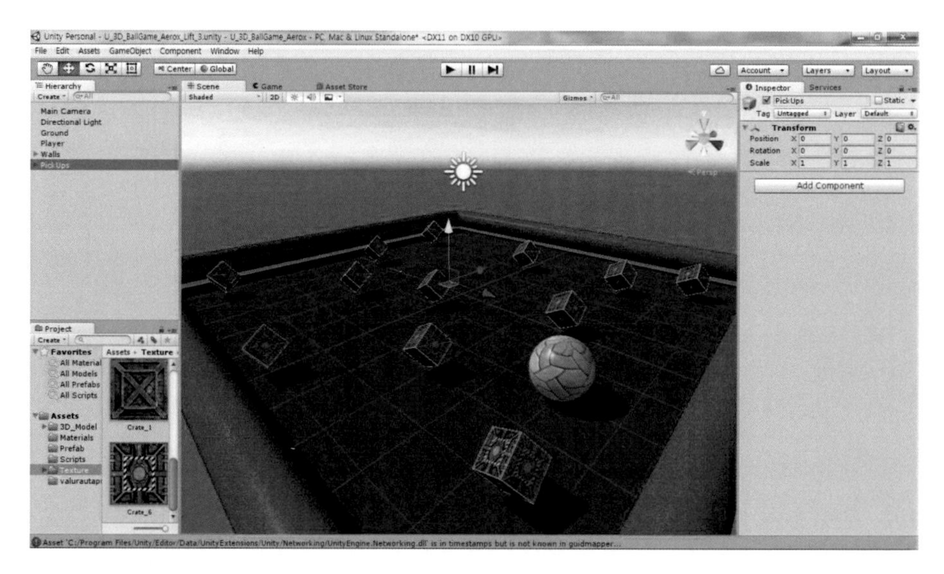

Fig 2. Pickup objects

15. Cube 형태의 pickup object를 Prefab 형태로 만드는 법

Cube 형태의 pickup object를 prefab 형태로 만드는 이유는 같은 기능을 가진 여러 개의 pickup object들이 사용되기 때문이다. 그래서 가장 기본이 되는 것을 prefab으로 만든 뒤에 여러 개로 복사를 하면 기능이 그대로 상속되어 나중에 수정하기가 쉽다.

먼저, 왼쪽 Project 〉 Assets 선택하고 나서, 왼쪽 Project 아래 〉 Create 〉 Folder 선택 〉 그러면 Assets folder 아래에 새 Folder 추가한다 〉 이름을 Prefab으로 수정한다 〉 왼쪽 Hierarchy에서 PickUp을 click & drag 형태로 끌어다가 왼쪽 Project 〉 Assets 〉 Prefab folder 안에다 넣는다.

왼쪽 Hierarchy 〉 Create 〉 Create Empty 선택 〉 Game Object 추가한다 〉 이름을 PickUps 로 수정한다 〉 새로 만든 PickUps 선택 〉 오른쪽 Inspector 〉 Transform rollout 오른쪽 톱니바퀴 click 〉 Reset 선택한다 〉 왼쪽 Hierarchy 〉 처음에 만들었던 PickUp을 click & drag 형태로 끌어다가 왼쪽 Hierarchy 아래에 새로 만든 PickUps 안으로 이동시킨다.

총 12개의 pickup object를 서로 다른 위치에다 만들기 위해서, 왼쪽 Hierarchy 〉 PickUps 〉 PickUp 선택 〉 Scene tab 위에 있는 Global과 Local 중에서 Global mode 선택되어 있는지 확인 〉 메뉴 Edit 〉 Duplicate 사용해서 복사 〉 아래와 같이 11개 복사해서 추가한다 〉 이때, Inspector의 Transform rollout 〉 Position 값들만 수정한다.

PickUp	0, 0.5, -5	PickUp(1)	4.5, 0.5, 4
PickUp(2)	4.5, 0.5, -4	PickUp(3)	-4, 0.5, 0
PickUp(4)	2, 0.5, -3	PickUp(5)	0, 0.5, 3
PickUp(6)	-2, 0.5, -2	PickUp(7)	-4.5, 0.5, 3
PickUp(8)	-4.5, 0.5, -4.5	PickUp(9)	0, 0.5, -1
PickUp(10)	3, 0.5, 0	PickUp(11)	3, 0.5, 3

참고로, red = X, green = Y, blue = Z 축을 의미한다. 게임을 실행해 보면, 12개의 pickup 육면체들이 똑같은 모습으로 회전한다.

16. Ball player가 PickUp item과의 충돌을 인식하도록 Tag를 지정하는 script 작성법

왼쪽 Project 〉 Assets 〉 Scripts 〉 PlayerController double click 〉 Visual Studio 열린다 〉 PlayerController 에서 아래와 같이 script를 추가한다.

〈Script #4〉

```
using UnityEngine;
using System.Collections;
using System.Collections.Generic;

public class PlayerController : MonoBehaviour {
    public float speed = 10.0f;       //1  moving speed of ball

    private Rigidbody rb;             //1  ball itself
    private float MoveHorizontal;
                                  //1  horizontal movement of ball
    private float MoveVertical;     //1  vertical movement of ball
    private Vector3 movement;        //1  final movement of ball

    // Use this for initialization
    void Start () {
```

```
        rb = GetComponent<Rigidbody>();  //1  ball itself
    }

    // Update is called once per frame
    void FixedUpdate () {  //1 FixedUpdate() instead of Update()

        // Get key inputs to make ball roll around
        MoveHorizontal = Input.GetAxis("Horizontal");
                              //1  horizontal movement of ball
        MoveVertical = Input.GetAxis("Vertical");
                              //1  vertical movement of ball

        movement = new Vector3(MoveHorizontal, 0.0f,
                    MoveVertical);  //1  final movement of ball
        rb.AddForce(movement * speed);
                    //1  modify direction of ball movement
    }

    //4 When collision happens with other, it is called
    void OnTriggerEnter(Collider Other) {
      //4  When ball hits something, this function is called
        //4  If ball player hits something with tag = "PickUp",
        if (Other.gameObject .CompareTag("PickUp"))  {
            Other.gameObject.SetActive(false);  //4  hide it
        }
```

```
    }
}
```

Script 작성 후에, Compile 하고 저장한다 〉 Visual Studio를 종료한다 〉 Unity Editor로 온다.

PickUp object의 tag를 수정하기 위해서, 왼쪽 Project 〉 Assets 〉 Prefab 〉 PickUp 선택한다 〉 오른쪽 Inspector 아래 3차원 6면체 icon 아래에 Tag = Untagged로 되어 있다.

Tag = untagged를 Tag = "PickUp"으로 수정하기 위해서, Tag = Untagged click 〉 "Add Tag" click 〉 Tags & Layers panel 나타난다 〉 Tags 아래에 있는 + click 〉 Tag0 나타난다 〉 그 옆의 New Tag를 PickUp으로 수정한다 〉 Save 버튼 click 한다 〉 다시 왼쪽 Project 〉 Assets 〉 Prefab 〉 PickUp 선택한다 〉 오른쪽 Inspector에서 보면 아직도 Tag = Untagged로 되어 있다 〉 Tag = Untagged click 〉 나타나는 list에서 맨 아래에 있는 PickUp 선택한다 〉 그러면 Tag = PickUp 으로 된다 〉 왼쪽 Hierarchy에서 〉 PickUps 〉 아래에 있는 12개 PickUp들을 각각 조사해 보면 Tag = PickUp 으로 수정되어 있다.

17. Ball player가 충돌을 일으켰을 때, 시야에서 안보이게 사라지도록 하는 법

왼쪽 Project 〉 Assets 〉 Prefab 〉 PickUp 선택한다 〉 오른쪽 Inspector 〉 Box Collider rollout 〉 Is Trigger 옆이 선택해제 되어 있다 〉 Is Trigger = true (선택) 한다 〉 그러면 자동으로 왼쪽 Hierarchy 〉

PickUps 〉 아래에 있는 12개 PickUp들의 Inspector 〉 Box Collider rollout 〉 Is Trigger = true (선택)로 된다 〉 Game 실행해서 ball player가 pickup cube들과 부딪치면 pickup들이 사라진다.

18. 화면에 score를 보이도록 Text를 사용하는 법

왼쪽 Hierarchy 〉 Create 〉 UI 〉 Text 선택한다 〉 그러면 Hierarchy 아래에 Canvas와 EventSystem 추가되고, Canvas 아래에 Text가 추가된다. 참고로, 화면에 Text를 추가하기 위해서는 Canvas와 EventSystem 두 개가 필요하다 〉 Canvas 아래에 있는 Text를 CountText로 수정한다 〉 오른쪽 Inspector 〉 Text(Script) rollout 〉 Color = white 흰색 선택, Font = Arial, Font Style = Normal, Font Size = 20, Text = Count Text로 수정한다.

CountText를 화면 왼쪽 위로 이동시키기 위해서, 왼쪽 Hierarchy 〉 Canvas 〉 CountText가 선택되어 있는 상태에서 〉 오른쪽 Inspector 〉 Rect Transform rollout 〉 왼쪽 위에 있는 빨간색 십자형 사각형 (= Anchor Preset) click 〉 여러 그림들이 보이는 Anchor Presets window가 나타난다 〉 Shift key와 Alt key를 동시에 누른 상태에서 왼쪽 위 모서리를 나타내는 그림 (= 왼쪽 윗부분에 있다) 인 Top & Left 영역 click 〉 그러면 Anchor Preset의 가운데 빨간 +가 왼쪽 위로 이동하게 되고, CountText는 화면 왼쪽 위 모서리에 위치하게 된다.

CountText를 화면 왼쪽 위 모서리에서 약간의 공간을 두도록 하기 위해서, 오른쪽 Inspector 〉 Rect Transform rollout 〉 Pos X = 30, Pos Y = -10, Pos Z = 0, Width = 160, Height = 30 으로 수정한다. 참고로,

이 값들은 일반 컴퓨터 모니터 해상도 1366x768에 맞춘 값들이다.

디자인 영역인 Scene tab 에서는 보이지 않지만 실제로 Game tab을 선택하고 게임을 play 해보면 화면 왼쪽 윗부분에 흰색 Count Text가 보인다.

19. 화면에 score를 보이도록 Ball player의 script인 PlayerController를 수정하는 법

왼쪽 Project 〉 Assets 〉 Scripts 〉 PlayerController double click 〉 Visual Studio 열린다 〉 PlayerController 에서 아래와 같이 script를 추가한다.

```
<Script #5>
using UnityEngine;
using UnityEngine.UI;        //5  Header file for text on screen

using System.Collections;
using System.Collections.Generic;

public class PlayerController : MonoBehaviour {

    public float speed = 10.0f;  //1  moving speed of ball
    public Text CountText;    //5  text on screen to show score

    private Rigidbody rb;  //1  ball itself
```

```
private float MoveHorizontal;
                              //1  horizontal movement of ball
private float MoveVertical;    //1  vertical movement of ball
private Vector3 movement;       //1  final movement of ball
private int count;
  //5  number of pickup items that the ball has collected

// Use this for initialization
void Start () {
    rb = GetComponent<Rigidbody>();  //1  ball itself
    count = 0;  //5  initial value
    CountText.text = "Count: " + count.ToString();
                                    //5  show count on screen
}

// Update is called once per frame
void FixedUpdate () {  //1 FixedUpdate() instead of Update()

    // Get key inputs to make ball roll around
    MoveHorizontal = Input.GetAxis("Horizontal");
                              //1  horizontal movement of ball
    MoveVertical = Input.GetAxis("Vertical");
                              //1  vertical movement of ball

    movement = new Vector3(MoveHorizontal, 0.0f,
```

```
                    MoveVertical);  //1  final movement of ball
        rb.AddForce(movement * speed);
                    //1  modify direction of ball movement
    }

    //4 When collision happens with other, it is called
    void OnTriggerEnter(Collider Other) {
      //4  When ball hits something, this function is called

        //4  If ball player hits something with tag = "PickUp",
        if (Other.gameObject .CompareTag("PickUp")) {
            Other.gameObject.SetActive(false);  //4  hide it

            count = count + 1;  //5  increase count by 1
            CountText.text = "Count: " + count.ToString();
                                    //5  update count on screen
        }
    }
}
```

Script 작성 후에, Compile하고 저장한다 〉 Visual Studio를 종료한다 〉 Unity Editor로 온다.

왼쪽 Hierarchy에서 Player 선택 〉 오른쪽 Inspector 〉 Player Controller(Script) 아래를 보면 Count Text 옆에 None(Text)로 되어 있

다 〉 왼쪽 Hierarchy에서 CountText를 click & drag 형태로 끌어다가 이 빈칸에 넣는다.

20. 화면에 message를 보이도록 Text를 사용하는 법
왼쪽 Hierarchy 〉 Create 〉 UI 〉 Text 선택한다 〉 그러면 Canvas 아래에 Text가 새로 추가된다. 참고로, 원래는 text를 추가하면 Canvas와 EventSystem이 추가되는데 우리는 조금 전에 CountText를 추가했기 때문에 이미 존재하는 Canvas 아래에 Text만 추가되었다.

Canvas 아래에 있는 Text를 GameOverText로 수정한다 〉 오른쪽 Inspector 〉 Text(Script) rollout 〉 Color = 분홍색 선택, Font = Arial, Font Style = Normal, Font Size = 40, Alignment = 둘 다 가운데로 선택, Text = Game Over !!! 로 수정한다. GameOverText 경우에는 화면 가운데를 중심으로 하고 있다. 그래서 Anchor Preset을 수정하지 않으므로 Anchor Preset의 가운데 빨간 +가 그대로 가운데에 있다.

GameOverText를 화면 정중앙에서 위로 약간 이동시키기 위해서, 오른쪽 Inspector 〉 Rect Transform rollout 〉 Pos X = 0, Pos Y = 60, Pos Z = 0, Width = 300, Height = 100 으로 수정한다. 참고로, 이 값들은 일반 컴퓨터 모니터 해상도 1366x768에 맞춘 값들이다.

21. 화면에 message가 보이도록 Ball player의 script인 Player Controller를 수정하는 법
왼쪽 Project 〉 Assets 〉 Scripts 〉 PlayerController double click 〉 Visual Studio 열린다 〉 PlayerController 에서 아래 script를 추가한다.

〈Script #6〉

```
using UnityEngine;
using UnityEngine.UI;        //5  Header file for text on screen
using System.Collections;

public class PlayerController : MonoBehaviour {
    public float speed = 10.0f;  //1  moving speed of ball
    public Text CountText;   //5  text on screen to show score
    public Text GameOverText;
            //6  text on screen to show "Game Over" message

    private Rigidbody rb;  //1  ball itself
    private float MoveHorizontal;
                        //1  horizontal movement of ball
    private float MoveVertical;    //1  vertical movement of ball
    private Vector3 movement;   //1  final movement of ball

    private int count;
     //5  number of pickup items that the ball has collected
    private int NumberOfPickUps = 12;
                            //6  number of pickup items

    // Use this for initialization
    void Start () {
        rb = GetComponent<Rigidbody>();  //1  ball itself
```

```
    count = 0;  //5  initial value
    CountText.text = "Count: " + count.ToString();
                                    //5  show count on screen
    GameOverText.text = ""  //6  message "Game Over !!!"
}

// Update is called once per frame
void FixedUpdate () {  //1 FixedUpdate() instead of Update()

    // Get key inputs to make ball roll around
    MoveHorizontal = Input.GetAxis("Horizontal");
                              //1  horizontal movement of ball
    MoveVertical = Input.GetAxis("Vertical");
                              //1  vertical movement of ball
    movement = new Vector3(MoveHorizontal, 0.0f,
                 MoveVertical);  //1  final movement of ball
    rb.AddForce(movement * speed);
                 //1  modify direction of ball movement
}

//4 When collision happens with other, it is called
void OnTriggerEnter(Collider Other) {
  //4  When ball hits something, this function is called

    //4  If ball player hits something with tag = "PickUp",
```

```
        if (Other.gameObject .CompareTag("PickUp")) {
            Other.gameObject.SetActive(false);  //4  hide it

            count = count + 1;  //5  increase count by 1
            CountText.text = "Count: " + count.ToString();
                                    //5  update count on screen
        }

        if (count == NumberOfPickUps)
             //6  If ball player has collected 12 pickup items,
        {
            GameOverText.text = "Game Over !!!"
                      //6  set GameOverText = "Game Over !!!"
        }
    }
}
```

Script 작성 후에, Compile하고 저장한다 〉 Visual Studio를 종료한다 〉 Unity Editor로 온다 〉 왼쪽 Hierarchy에서 Player 선택 〉 오른쪽 Inspector 〉 Player Controller (Script) 아래를 보면 GameOverText 옆에 None으로 되어 있다 〉 왼쪽 Hierarchy에서 GameOverText를 click & drag 형태로 끌어다가 이 빈칸에 넣는다. 참고로, Scene mode에서 Game mode로 전환하면 게임 실행 전에 "Count Text"와 "Game Over !!!"가 보일 수도 있는데 이것은 게임 실행전이기 때문에 디자인 내용이 보이는 것이다. 게임을 실행하면 사라진다.

22. Game 완성한 뒤에 web 상에서 사용하는 방법

메뉴 File 〉 Save Scene 선택해서 저장한다 〉 메뉴 File 〉 Build Settings 선택 〉 Build Setting window 나타난다 〉 왼쪽 Platform에서 WebGL 선택 〉 아래의 Switch Platform button click 〉 그러면 WebGL 선택되면서 Unity icon이 그 옆에 표시된다 〉 가운데 오른쪽에 있는 Add Open Scenes button click 〉 그러면 지금 만들고 있는 game이 위의 Scenes In Build 영역에 추가된다 〉 오른쪽 아래에 있는 Build And Run button click 〉 저장할 folder를 지정하기 위해서 C:\ user \ My Documents \ U_3D_BallGame \ 아래에다 WebGL 이라는 이름의 새 folder를 하나 만들고 나서 지금 새로 만든 WebGL folder를 선택해서 지정한다. 참고로, web 경우에는 *.html가 만들어지고, PC로 하면 *.exe가 만들어진다. 그리고 실행하려고 할 때, Unity Web Player가 필요하다면 download 하고 실행하면 된다. 마지막으로, web 상에서 게임 실행을 끝내려면 web page를 닫는다.

Windows 용으로 만들려면, 왼쪽 Platform에서 PC, Mac, Linux Stand Alone 선택 〉 아래의 Switch Platform button click 〉 나머지는 위와 같다. Windows 용은 바로 실행이 되는데 Configuration window가 나타나면 아래 오른쪽에 있는 windowed를 선택한다. 그래야 나중에 게임이 끝나고 나서 창을 닫을 수 있다.

23. Timer가 보이도록 Text를 사용하는 법

왼쪽 Hierarchy 〉 Create 〉 UI 〉 Text 선택한다 〉 Hierarchy 〉 Canvas 아래에 Text가 추가된다. Canvas 아래에 있는 Text를 TimerText로 수정한다 〉 오른쪽 Inspector 〉 Text (Script) rollout 〉

Color = 흰색 선택, Font = Arial, Font Style = Normal, Font Size = 20, Alignment = 둘 다 왼쪽 것으로 선택, Text = Timer Text로 수정한다.

TimerText를 화면 오른쪽 위로 이동시키기 위해서, 오른쪽 Inspector 〉 Rect Transform rollout 〉 왼쪽 위에 있는 사각형 (= Anchor Preset) click 〉 Shift key와 Alt key를 동시에 누른 상태에서 Top & Right 영역 click 〉 그러면 Anchor Preset의 가운데 빨간 +가 오른쪽 위로 이동하게 되고, TimerText는 화면 오른쪽 위 모서리에 위치하게 된다.

TimerText를 화면 오른쪽 위 모서리에서 약간의 공간을 두도록 하기 위해서, 오른쪽 Inspector 〉 Rect Transform rollout 〉 Pos X = 0, Pos Y = -10, Pos Z = 0, Width = 230, Height = 30 으로 수정한다. Game tab을 선택하면 오른쪽 위에 Timer Text가 보인다. 참고로, 이전에 만든 CountText 에서는 width = 160이었다. 이번에 TimerText = 230 인 이유는 시간을 표시해야 하므로 더 넓은 영역이 필요하기 때문이다. 참고로, 이 값들은 일반 컴퓨터 모니터 해상도 1366x768에 맞춘 값들이다.

24. Game play 시간이 바뀌면서 정지하도록 PlayerController를 수정하는 법

왼쪽 Project 〉 Assets 〉 Scripts 〉 PlayerController double click 〉 Visual Studio 열린다 〉 PlayerController 에서 script를 추가한다.

〈Script #7〉

```
using UnityEngine;
```

```
using UnityEngine.UI;       //5  Header file for text on screen
using System.Collections;
using System.Collections.Generic;

public class PlayerController : MonoBehaviour {
    public float speed = 10.0f;  //1  moving speed of ball
    public Text CountText;   //5  text on screen to show score
    public Text GameOverText;
            //6  text on screen to show "Game Over" message
    public Text TimerText;   //7  text on screen to show timer

    private Rigidbody rb;  //1  ball itself
    private float MoveHorizontal;
                          //1  horizontal movement of ball
    private float MoveVertical;
                          //1  vertical movement of ball
    private Vector3 movement;    //1  final movement of ball
    private int count;
     //5  number of pickup items that the ball has collected
    private int NumberOfPickUps = 12;
                               //6  number of pickup items
    private float StartTime;        //7  starting time
    private bool GameHasFinished = false
                    //7  condition if game has finished or not
    private float ElapsedTime;
```

```
        //7  elapsed time = current time - start time
private string Minutes;       //7  minutes
private string Seconds;       //7  seconds

// Use this for initialization
void Start () {
    rb = GetComponent<Rigidbody>();  //1  ball itself

    count = 0;  //5  initial value
    CountText.text = "Count: " + count.ToString();
                                //5  show count on screen
    GameOverText.text = ""  //6  message "Game Over !!!“

    StartTime = Time.time;              //7  starting time
    TimerText.color = Color.yellow;
                        //7  set timer color to yellow
}
// Update is called once per frame
void FixedUpdate () {  //1 FixedUpdate() instead of Update()

    // Get key inputs to make ball roll around
    MoveHorizontal = Input.GetAxis("Horizontal");
                        //1  horizontal movement of ball
    MoveVertical = Input.GetAxis("Vertical");
                        //1  vertical movement of ball
```

```
    movement = new Vector3(MoveHorizontal, 0.0f,
                MoveVertical);  //1  final movement of ball
    rb.AddForce(movement * speed);
                //1  modify direction of ball movement

    if (GameHasFinished == false)
        //7  while ball is collecting 12 pickup items,
    {
        ElapsedTime = Time.time - StartTime;
         //7  elapsed time = current time - start time
        Minutes = ((int)ElapsedTime / 60).ToString();
        Seconds = (ElapsedTime % 60).ToString("f0");
                //7  "f0" means integer value format for
                    // seconds, not float value format
        TimerText.text = "Elapsed Time: " + Minutes + "M "
                    + Seconds + "S";
                    //7  show elapsed time on screen
    }
}

//4 When collision happens with other, it is called
void OnTriggerEnter(Collider Other) {
  //4  When ball hits something, this function is called
    /4  If ball player hits something with tag = "PickUp",
    if (Other.gameObject .CompareTag("PickUp")) {
```

```
            Other.gameObject.SetActive(false);  //4  hide it
            count = count + 1;  //5  increase count by 1
            CountText.text = "Count: " + count.ToString();
                                //5  update count on screen
        }

        if (count == NumberOfPickUps)
              //6  If ball player has collected 12 pickup items,
        {
            GameOverText.text = "Game Over !!!"
                        //6  set GameOverText = "Game Over !!!"

            GameHasFinished = true
              //7  Game has finished because the ball has
              //      collected all 12 pickup items
            TimerText.color = Color.red;
                                //7  change timer color to red
        }
    }
}
```

Script 작성 후에, Compile하고 저장한다 〉 Visual Studio를 종료한다 〉 Unity Editor로 온다 〉 왼쪽 Hierarchy에서 Player 선택 〉 오른쪽 Inspector 〉 Player Controller (Script) 아래를 보면 Timer Text 옆에 None으로 되어 있다 〉 왼쪽 Hierarchy에서 TimerText를 click & drag

형태로 끌어다가 이 빈칸에 넣는다. 참고로, Visual Studio에서 컴파일 했는데 문제가 발생했다고 하면서 UnityEngine.UI가 존재하지 않는다는 메시지가 나올 수 있다. 그냥 무시하고 저장하고 Unity Editor로 가서 실행하면 제대로 된다. 발생하는 에러 메시지는 The type or namespace name "UI" does not exist in the namespace "UnityEngine" (are you missing an assembly reference?) 이다

25. Cube 사용하여 bar 형태의 장애물 추가하기

추가할 Block이 35개 이므로 이것들을 담을 Blocks라는 이름의 빈 folder를 하나 만들기 위해서, 메뉴 Game Object 〉 Create Empty 선택 〉 Hierarchy에 Game Object 추가된다 〉 추가된 Game Object의 이름을 Blocks로 수정한다 〉 Blocks 선택 〉 오른쪽 Inspector 〉 Transform rollout 〉 오른쪽 톱니바퀴 click 〉 Reset 선택한다 〉 그러면 아래 숫자들이 초기화 된다. 참고로, 앞으로 만들어질 Block 35개는 Blocks의 위치에서 상대적으로 만들어지므로 Blocks의 위치를 reset 시키는 것은 매우 중요한 일이다.

Block으로 사용할 Cube를 추가하기 위해서, 메뉴 Game Object 〉 3D Object 〉 Cube 선택 〉 Hierarchy에서 이름을 Block으로 한다 〉 Block를 집어다가 Blocks 아래로 넣는다 〉 오른쪽 Inspector 〉 Transform rollout 〉 아래의 숫자들을 -1, 0.5, 0, 0, 0, 0, 0.8, 1, 0.8 로 수정한다 〉 Brick_4.png를 import 한 뒤에 Texture를 입혀 기본이 되는 block을 만든다.

왼쪽 Hierarchy 〉 Blocks 아래에 있는 Block 선택 〉 메뉴 Edit 〉

Copy와 Paste 명령어를 사용하여 아래와 같은 위치에 복사해서 놓는다.

Bar(8) -1, 0.5, 0,	Bar(12) -3, 0.5, -4,
Bar(14) 3, 0.5, -1,	Bar(15) -3, 0.5, -3,
Bar(16) -4, 0.5, -3,	Bar(17) -1, 0.5, -4,
Bar(18) -1, 0.5, -3,	Bar(19) -4, 0.5, -1,
Bar(20) -3, 0.5, -1,	Bar(21) -2, 0.5, -1,
Bar(22) -1, 0.5, -1,	Bar(23) 1, 0.5, -4,
Bar(24) 1, 0.5, -3,	Bar(25) 1, 0.5, -2,
Bar(26) 1, 0.5, -1,	Bar(27) 3, 0.5, -3,
Bar(28) 3, 0.5, -4,	Bar(29) -3, 0.5, 1,
Bar(30) -4, 0.5, 1,	Bar(31) -1, 0.5, -1,
Bar(32) -1, 0.5, 2,	Bar(33) -2, 0.5, 2,
Bar(34) -3, 0.5, 2,	Bar(35) -4, 0.5, 2,
Bar(36) -3, 0.5, 4,	Bar(37) -2, 0.5, 4,
Bar(38) -1, 0.5, 4,	Bar(39) 3, 0.5, 4,
Bar(40) 2, 0.5, 4,	Bar(41) 1, 0.5, 4,
Bar(42) 1, 0.5, 1,	Bar(43) 2, 0.5, 1,
Bar(44) 2, 0.5, 2,	Bar(45) 1, 0.5, 2,
Bar(46) 4, 0.5, 2,	Bar(47) 4, 0.5, 1,

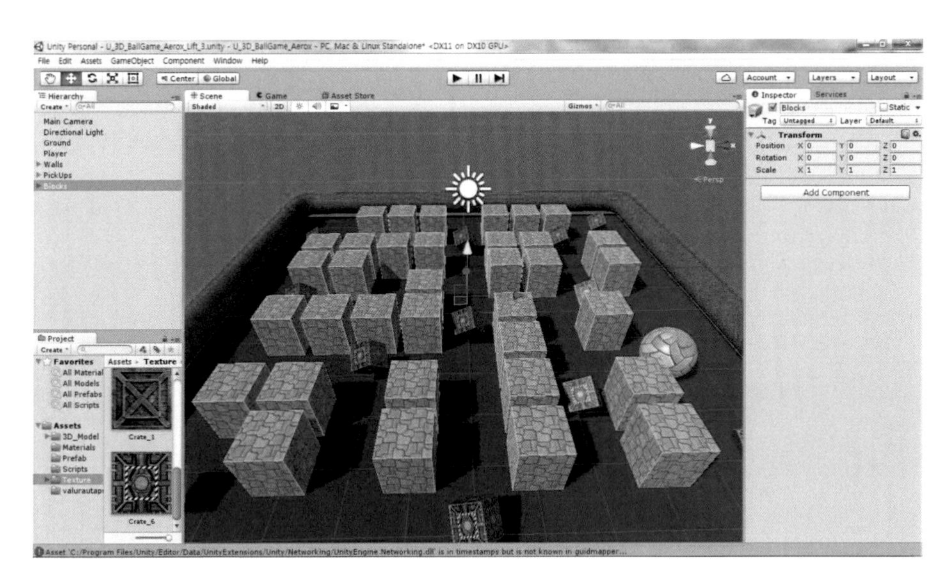
Hierarchy
Main Camera
Directional Light
Ground
Player
Walls
PickUps
Blocks
Scene
Game
Asset Store
Inspector
Services
Transform
Position
Rotation
Scale
Add Component
Project
Favorites
Assets
3D_Model
Materials
Prefab
Scripts
Texture
Crate_1
Crate_6

Fig 3. Blocks

26. Ghost를 추가하는 법

메뉴 Game Object 〉 3D Object 〉 Sphere 선택한다 〉 이름을 Ghost로 수정한다 〉 오른쪽 Inspector 〉 Transform rollout 〉 -4.5, 0.5, 4.5, 0, 0, 0, 1, 1, 1로 수정한다.

Ghost가 자기 스스로 움직일 수 있도록 하기 위해서, 왼쪽 Hierarchy 〉 Ghost 선택 〉 오른쪽 Inspector 〉 맨 아래 Add Component button click 〉 Physics 〉 Rigid Body 선택 〉 Rigid Body Component 추가된다. 참고로, Use Gravity = true (선택)로 초기값이 설정되어 있다.

27. Ghost에 대한 script 작성하는 법

왼쪽 Hierarchy 〉 Ghost 선택 〉 오른쪽 Inspector 〉 맨 아래 Add Component button click 〉 맨 아래 New Scripts 선택 〉 Name = Ghost로 쓴다 〉 C# 선택 〉 Create and Add button click한다 〉 그러면 왼쪽 아래 Project 〉 Assets folder 아래에 Ghost 추가된다 〉 이것을 집어다가 Scripts folder 안으로 이동시킨다.

Script를 작성하기 위해서, Project 〉 Assets folder 〉 Scripts folder 〉 Ghost를 double click 〉 그러면 Visual Studio가 실행된다 〉 아래 script를 작성한다.

〈Script #8〉

```
using UnityEngine;
using System.Collections;
using System.Collections.Generic;

public class Ghost : MonoBehaviour {
    public Transform target;
              //8  target is the ball player that ghost will follow
    public float speed = 0.05f;  //8  moving speed of the ghost

    // Use this for initialization
    void Start () {

    }

    // Update is called once per frame
    void FixedUpdate () {  //8 FixedUpdate() instead of Update()
        if (transform.position != target.position)
              //8  if the position of ghost is not same to that
              //      of the ball player
        {
            transform.position =
              Vector3.MoveTowards(transform.position,
              target.position, speed);
              //8  update the position of ghost by making the
              //      ghost move toward to the position of the
```

```
                    //      ball player with the specified speed
            }
        }
    }
```

Script 작성 후에, Compile하고 저장한다 〉 Visual Studio를 종료한다 〉 Unity Editor로 온다. 왼쪽 Hierarchy에서 Ghost 선택 〉 오른쪽 Inspector 〉 Ghost (Script) 아래를 보면 Target 옆에 None으로 되어 있다 〉 왼쪽 Hierarchy에서 Player를 click & drag 형태로 끌어다가 이 빈 칸에 넣는다.

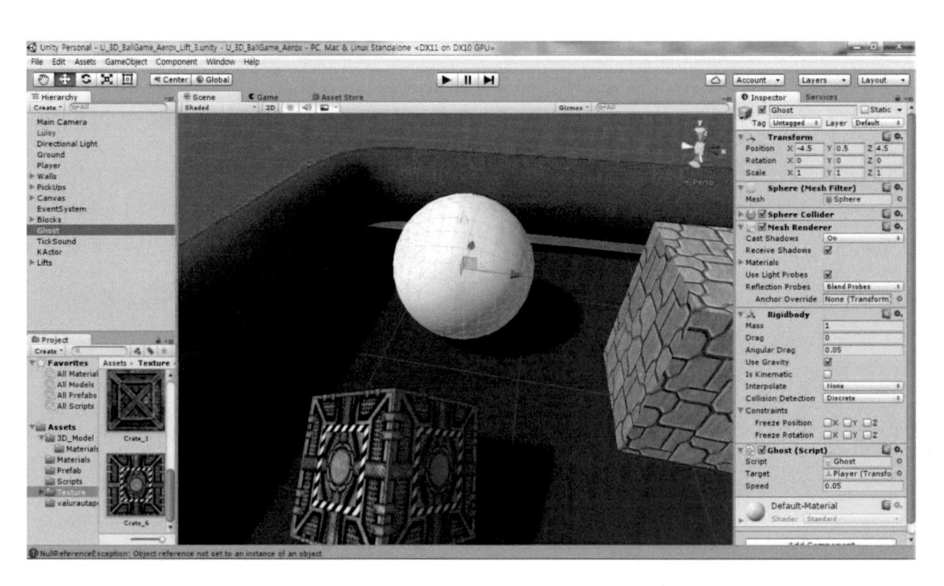

Fig 4. Ghost

28. 충돌할 때, Wave file 실행하는 법

메뉴 Assets 〉 Import New Asset 〉 Tickwave.wav file 선택한다 〉 그

러면, Project 〉 Assets 〉 아래에 추가된다 〉 Tickwave.wav file을 집어다가 Hierarchy에 추가시킨다 〉 이름을 TickSound로 수정한다 〉 그러면 자동으로 오른쪽 Inspector에 Audio Source component가 추가된다 〉 Hierarchy에서 TickSound 선택한다 〉 오른쪽 Inspector 〉 Audio Source component 〉 Play On Awake = false (선택 해제) 시킨다. 참고로, 이것을 선택해제 해야 처음에 시작할 때 자동으로 소리가 나지 않는다.

왼쪽 Project 〉 Assets 〉 Scripts 〉 PlayerController double click 〉 Visual Studio 열린다 〉 PlayerController 에서 아래와 같이 script를 추가한다.

```
<Script #9>
using UnityEngine;
using UnityEngine.UI;        //5  Header file for text on screen
using System.Collections;
using System.Collections.Generic;

public class PlayerController : MonoBehaviour {
    public float speed = 10.0f;     //1  moving speed of ball
    public Text CountText;    //5  text on screen to show score
    public Text GameOverText;
            //6  text on screen to show "Game Over" message
    public Text TimerText;
                        //7  text on screen to show timer
```

```
public AudioSource TickSound;
                        //9  wave file to make sound when
                        //        player hits a pickup item

private Rigidbody rb;  //1  ball itself
private float MoveHorizontal;
                        //1  horizontal movement of ball
private float MoveVertical;     //1  vertical movement of ball
private Vector3 movement;   //1  final movement of ball
private int count;
                        //5  number of pickup items that
                        //        the ball has collected
private int NumberOfPickUps = 12;
                        //6  number of pickup items

private float StartTime;      //7  starting time
private bool GameHasFinished = false
                    //7  condition if game has finished or not
private float ElapsedTime;
          //7  elapsed time = current time - start time
private string Minutes;       //7  minutes
private string Seconds;       //7  seconds

//9  Make a wave file ready to play
void Awake()  //9  Make a wave file ready to play
```

```
    {
        if (TickSound == null)
                    //9  if TickSound file is not ready to play,
        {
            TickSound = GameObject.Find("TickSound").
             GetComponent<AudioSource>();
             //9  find it in Hierarchy and make it ready to play
        }
    }

    // Use this for initialization
    void Start () {
        rb = GetComponent<Rigidbody>();  //1  ball itself
        count = 0;  //5  initial value
        CountText.text = "Count: " + count.ToString();
                                     //5  show count on screen
        GameOverText.text = ""  //6  message "Game Over !!!"
        StartTime = Time.time;              //7  starting time
        TimerText.color = Color.yellow;
                              //7  set timer color to yellow
}

// Update is called once per frame
void FixedUpdate () {  //1 FixedUpdate() instead of Update()
        // Get key inputs to make ball roll around
```

```
        MoveHorizontal = Input.GetAxis("Horizontal");
                              //1  horizontal movement of ball
        MoveVertical = Input.GetAxis("Vertical");
                              //1  vertical movement of ball

        movement = new Vector3(MoveHorizontal, 0.0f,
                   MoveVertical);  //1  final movement of ball
        rb.AddForce(movement * speed);
                   //1  modify direction of ball movement

        if (GameHasFinished == false)
             //7  while ball is collecting 12 pickup items,
        {
            ElapsedTime = Time.time - StartTime;
             //7  elapsed time = current time - start time
            Minutes = ((int)ElapsedTime / 60).ToString();
            Seconds = (ElapsedTime % 60).ToString("f0");
                   //7  "f0" means integer value format for
                   //      seconds, not float value format
            TimerText.text = "Elapsed Time: " + Minutes + "M "
                                   + Seconds + "S";
                   //7  show elapsed time on screen
        }
}
    //4 When collision happens with other, it is called
```

```
void OnTriggerEnter(Collider Other) {
  //4  When ball hits something, this function is called

    //4  If ball player hits something with tag = "PickUp",
    if (Other.gameObject .CompareTag("PickUp")) {
        Other.gameObject.SetActive(false);  //4  hide it
        count = count + 1;  //5  increase count by 1
        CountText.text = "Count: " + count.ToString();
                          //5  update count on screen

        TickSound.Play();  //9  play TickSound file when
                          //   ball player hits a pickup item
    }

    if (count == NumberOfPickUps)
         //6  If ball player has collected 12 pickup items,
    {
        GameOverText.text = "Game Over !!!"
                  //6  set GameOverText = "Game Over !!!"

        GameHasFinished = true
                  //7  Game has finished because the ball
                  //     has collected all 12 pickup items
        TimerText.color = Color.red;
                          //7  change timer color to red
```

```
            }
        }
    }
```

Script 작성 후에, Compile하고 저장한다 〉 Visual Studio 를 종료한다 〉 Unity Editor로 온다 〉 왼쪽 Hierarchy에서 Player 선택 〉 오른쪽 Inspector 〉 Player Controller (Script) 아래를 보면 Tick Sound 옆에 None으로 되어 있다 〉 왼쪽 Hierarchy에서 TickSound를 click & drag 형태로 끌어다가 이 빈칸에 넣는다.

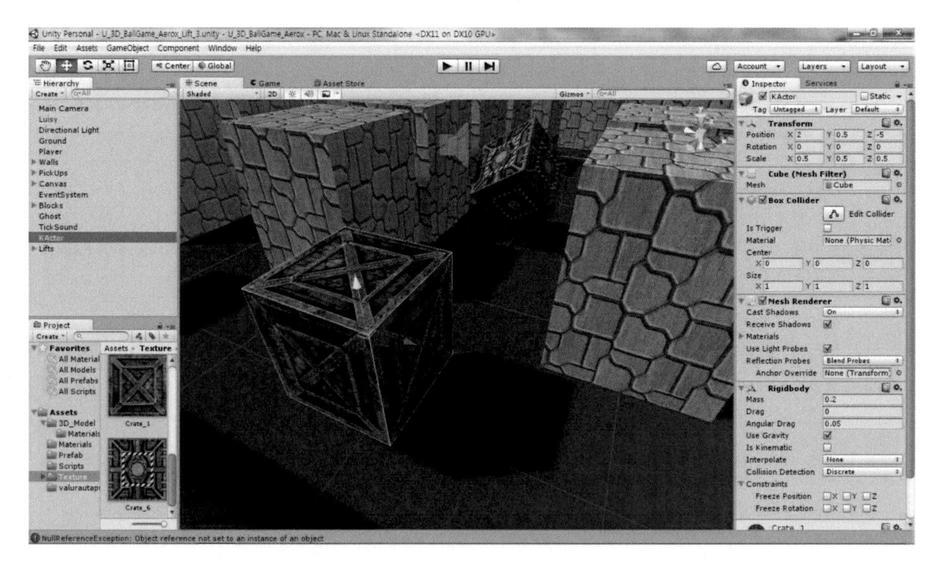

Fig 5. Kactor

29. 물리적 역학이 적용하는 KActor 추가하는 법

메뉴 Game Object 〉 3D Object 〉 Cube 추가한다 〉 왼쪽 Hierarchy 〉 Cube 선택 〉 이름을 KActor로 수정한다 〉 오른쪽 Inspector 〉

Transform rollout 〉 아래 값들을 3, 0.5, -5, 0, 0, 0, 0.5, 0.5, 0.5로 수정한다 〉 오른쪽 Inspector 〉 Add Component 〉 Physics 〉 Rigid Body 〉 Rigid Body Component 추가된다 〉 참고로, Use Gravity = true (선택)로 되어 있다 〉 Mass = 0.2로 해서 가볍게 만든다 〉 원하는 texture를 입힌다. 참고로, KActor는 script가 필요하지 않다.

30. Ball player를 정지시키는 법

PlayerController script에서 아래와 같이 수정한다.

```
〈Script #10〉
using UnityEngine;
using UnityEngine.UI;        //5  Header file for text on screen
using System.Collections;

public class PlayerController : MonoBehaviour {
    public float speed = 10.0f;     //1  moving speed of ball
    public Text CountText;    //5  text on screen to show score
    public Text GameOverText;
              //6  text on screen to show "Game Over" message
    public Text TimerText;    //7  text on screen to show timer
    public AudioSource TickSound;  //9  wave file to make
                    // sound when player hits a pickup item

    private Rigidbody rb;  //1  ball itself
    private float MoveHorizontal;
```

```
                    //1  horizontal movement of ball
private float MoveVertical;    //1  vertical movement of ball
private Vector3 movement;   //1  final movement of ball
private int count;
  //5  number of pickup items that the ball has collected
private int NumberOfPickUps = 12;
                                //6  number of pickup items

private float StartTime;                //7  starting time
private bool GameHasFinished = false
                //7  condition if game has finished or not
private float ElapsedTime;
          //7  elapsed time = current time - start time
private string Minutes;      //7  minutes
private string Seconds;      //7  seconds
private bool held_Q;  //10  input key 'Q' to make ball stop

//9  Make wave file ready to play
void Awake()  //9  Make wave file ready to play
{
    if (TickSound == null)
                //9  if TickSound file is not ready to play,
    {
        TickSound = GameObject.Find("TickSound").
         GetComponent<AudioSource>();
```

```
            //9  find it in Hierarchy and make it ready to play
        }
    }

    // Use this for initialization
    void Start () {
        rb = GetComponent<Rigidbody>();  //1  ball itself
        count = 0;  //5  initial value
        CountText.text = "Count: " + count.ToString();
                                         //5  show count on screen

        GameOverText.text = ""  //6  message "Game Over !!!"
        StartTime = Time.time;             //7  starting time
        TimerText.color = Color.yellow;
                                  //7  set timer color to yellow
    }

    // Update is called once per frame
    void FixedUpdate () {  //1 FixedUpdate() instead of Update()

        // Get key inputs to make ball roll around
        MoveHorizontal = Input.GetAxis("Horizontal");
                                  //1  horizontal movement of ball
        MoveVertical = Input.GetAxis("Vertical");
                                  //1  vertical movement of ball
```

```
    movement = new Vector3(MoveHorizontal, 0.0f,
                MoveVertical);  //1  final movement of ball
    rb.AddForce(movement * speed);
                //1  modify direction of ball movement

    if (GameHasFinished == false)
        //7  while ball is collecting 12 pickup items,
    {
        ElapsedTime = Time.time - StartTime;
         //7  elapsed time = current time - start time
        Minutes = ((int)ElapsedTime / 60).ToString();
        Seconds = (ElapsedTime % 60).ToString("f0");
        TimerText.text = "Elapsed Time: " + Minutes + "M "
         + Seconds + "S"; //7  show elapsed time on screen
    }

    //10 Press 'Q' key to make the ball player stop
    held_Q = Input.GetKey(KeyCode.Q);
    if (held_Q == true) rb.velocity = Vector3.zero;
        //10  If 'Q key is pressed, make the ball stop
}

//4 When collision happens with other, it is called
void OnTriggerEnter(Collider Other) {
  //4  When ball hits something, this function is called
```

```
        //4  If ball player hits something with tag = "PickUp",
        if (Other.gameObject .CompareTag("PickUp")) {
            Other.gameObject.SetActive(false);  //4  hide it
            count = count + 1;  //5  increase count by 1
            CountText.text = "Count: " + count.ToString();
                                    //5  update count on screen
            TickSound.Play();  //9  play TickSound file when
                              //     ball player hits a pickup item
        }

        if (count == NumberOfPickUps)
              //6  If ball player has collected 12 pickup items,
        {
            GameOverText.text = "Game Over !!!"
                      //6  set GameOverText = "Game Over !!!"

            GameHasFinished = true    //7  Game has finished
            TimerText.color = Color.red;
                              //7  change timer color to red
        }
    }
}
```

31. 'Ghost를 사라지게 하는 법

Ghost script에서 아래와 같이 수정한다.

<Script #11>

```
using UnityEngine;
using System.Collections;

public class Ghost : MonoBehaviour {
    public Transform target;
            //8  target is the ball player that ghost will follow
    public float speed = 0.05f;  //8  moving speed of the ghost
    private bool held_X;  //11  input key 'X' to destroy Ghost

    // Use this for initialization
    void Start () {
    }

    // Update is called once per frame
    void FixedUpdate () {  //8 FixedUpdate() instead of Update()
        if (transform.position != target.position) {
            //8  if the position of ghost is not same to that of
            //the ball player
          transform.position = Vector3.MoveTowards(
            transform.position, target.position, speed);
        }

      //11  Press 'X' to destroy Ghost
        held_X = Input.GetKey(KeyCode.X);
```

```
            if (held_X == true) Destroy(gameObject);
                //11  if 'X' key is pressed, destroy Ghost
        }
    }
```

32. 반복적으로 움직이는 Auto Lift 만드는 법

참고로, Auto Lift는 Ball player와는 아무런 상관없이 자기 스스로 계속 움직인다. 그런데 위/아래로 움직인다고 해서 RigidBody 형태가 아니다. 단순히 기본적인 GameObject Cube 형태이다.

앞으로 만들 Lift가 3종류이므로 이것들을 담을 Lifts라는 이름의 빈 folder를 하나 만들기 위해서, 메뉴 Game Object 〉 Create Empty 선택 〉 Hierarchy에 Game Object 추가된다 〉 추가된 Game Object의 이름을 Lifts로 수정한다 〉 Lifts 선택 〉 오른쪽 Inspector 〉 Transform rollout 〉 오른쪽 톱니바퀴 click 〉 Reset 선택한다 〉 그러면 아래 숫자들이 초기화 된다.

메뉴 Game Object 〉 3D Object 〉 Cube 선택한다 〉 이름을 AutoLift_1로 수정한다 〉 AutoLift_1를 집어다가 Lifts 아래로 넣는다 〉 오른쪽 Inspector 〉 Transform rollout 〉 5, 0.5, -5, 0, 0, 0, 1, 1, 1로 수정한다 〉 원하는 texture를 입힌다.

AutoLift_1가 자동으로 움직이도록 Script를 작성하기 위해서, Project 〉 Assets folder 〉 Scripts folder 〉 PlayerController를 double click 〉 그러면 Visual Studio가 실행된다 〉 아래 script를 작성한다.

참고로, PlayerController 에다 script를 작성하는 이유는 나머지 다른 종류 Lift들은 ball player와의 거리에 상관하기 때문이다.

```
〈Script #12〉
using UnityEngine;
using UnityEngine.UI;        //5  Header file for text on screen
using System.Collections;

public class PlayerController : MonoBehaviour {
    const int UP = 1;                    //12, 13  UP direction
    const int DOWN = -1;                 //12, 13  DOWN direction
    public float speed = 10.0f;          //1  moving speed of ball
    public Text CountText;    //5  text on screen to show score
    public Text GameOverText;
              //6  text on screen to show "Game Over" message

    public Text TimerText;    //7  text on screen to show timer
    public AudioSource TickSound;
                             //9  wave file to make sound when
                             //     player hits a pickup item
    public GameObject AutoLift_1;
                   //12  Auto Lift #1 at the right front corner

    private Rigidbody rb;  //1  ball itself
    private float MoveHorizontal;
```

```
                    //1  horizontal movement of ball
private float MoveVertical;    //1  vertical movement of ball
private Vector3 movement;    //1  final movement of ball
private int count;
  //5  number of pickup items that the ball has collected
private int NumberOfPickUps = 12;
                              //6  number of pickup items

private float StartTime;                //7  starting time
private bool GameHasFinished = false
                 //7  condition if game has finished or not
private float ElapsedTime;
         //7  elapsed time = current time - start time
private string Minutes;     //7  minutes
private string Seconds;     //7  seconds
private bool held_Q;  //10  input key 'Q' to make ball stop

private int AutoLift_1_Direction = -1;
         //12  initial direction of AutoLift_1 is down,
         //      where 1 = up and -1 = down
private float AutoLift_1_BottomLimit = -0.4f;
         //12  bottom limit of movement of AutoLift_1
private float AutoLift_1_TopLimit = 0.5f;
         //12  top limit of movement of AutoLift_1
//9  Make a wave file ready to play
```

```
void Awake()  //9  Make a wave file ready to play
{
    if (TickSound == null)
                //9  if TickSound file is not ready to play,
    {
        TickSound = GameObject.Find("TickSound").
         GetComponent<AudioSource>();
         //9  find it in Hierarchy and make it ready to play
    }
}

// Use this for initialization
void Start () {
    rb = GetComponent<Rigidbody>();  //1  ball itself

    count = 0;  //5  initial value
    CountText.text = "Count: " + count.ToString();
                                    //5  show count on screen
    GameOverText.text = ""          //6  message "Game Over !!!"

    StartTime = Time.time;                  //7  starting time
    TimerText.color = Color.yellow;
                              //7  set timer color to yellow
}
```

```
// Update is called once per frame
void FixedUpdate () {  //1 FixedUpdate() instead of Update()

    // Get key inputs to make ball roll around
    MoveHorizontal = Input.GetAxis("Horizontal");
                        //1  horizontal movement of ball
    MoveVertical = Input.GetAxis("Vertical");
                        //1  vertical movement of ball
    movement = new Vector3(MoveHorizontal, 0.0f,
                MoveVertical);  //1  final movement of ball
    rb.AddForce(movement * speed);
                //1  modify direction of ball movement

    if (GameHasFinished == false)
        //7  while ball is collecting 12 pickup items,
    {
        ElapsedTime = Time.time - StartTime;
         //7  elapsed time = current time - start time
        Minutes = ((int)ElapsedTime / 60).ToString();
        Seconds = (ElapsedTime % 60).ToString("f0");
        TimerText.text = "Elapsed Time: " + Minutes + "M "
                + Seconds + "S";
                        //7  show elapsed time on screen
    }
    //10 Press 'Q' key to make the ball player stop
```

```
        held_Q = Input.GetKey(KeyCode.Q);  //10
        if (held_Q == true) rb.velocity = Vector3.zero;
                        //10  If 'Q key pressed, make the ball stop

        // 12  C A L L     M A T I N E E
        UF_MATINEE();  //12  call UF_MATINEE() for all lifts
    }

//4 When collision happens with other, it is called
void OnTriggerEnter(Collider Other) {
  //4  When ball hits something, this function is called

        //4  If ball player hits something with tag = "PickUp",
        if (Other.gameObject .CompareTag("PickUp")) {
            Other.gameObject.SetActive(false);  //4  hide it
            count = count + 1;  //5  increase count by 1
            CountText.text = "Count: " + count.ToString();
                            //5  update count on screen

            TickSound.Play();  //9  play TickSound file when
                            //     ball player hits a pickup item
        }

        if (count == NumberOfPickUps)
            //6  If ball player has collected 12 pickup items,
```

```
    {
        GameOverText.text = "Game Over !!!"
                //6  set GameOverText = "Game Over !!!"

        GameHasFinished = true
                //7  Game has finished because the ball
                //      has collected all 12 pickup items
        TimerText.color = Color.red;
                //7  change timer color to red
    }
}

// 12  M A T I N E E
void UF_MATINEE() {
    //12  AutoLift_1 - automatic lift moving up and down
    //    in the range of [AutoLift_1_BottomLimit ..
    //    AutoLift_1_TopLimit]
    if ((AutoLift_1_Direction == 1) &&
         (AutoLift_1.transform.position.y <
                AutoLift_1_TopLimit))
         AutoLift_1.transform.position =
                AutoLift_1.transform.position +
                     new Vector3(0.0f, 0.01f, 0.0f);

    if ((AutoLift_1_Direction == 1) &&
```

```
            (AutoLift_1.transform.position.y >=
                    AutoLift_1_TopLimit))
                    AutoLift_1_Direction = -1 *
                            AutoLift_1_Direction;

        if ((AutoLift_1_Direction == -1) &&
            (AutoLift_1.transform.position.y >
                    AutoLift_1_BottomLimit))
                    AutoLift_1.transform.position =
                    AutoLift_1.transform.position +
                            new Vector3(0.0f, -0.01f, 0.0f);

        if ((AutoLift_1_Direction == -1) &&
            (AutoLift_1.transform.position.y <=
                    AutoLift_1_BottomLimit))
                    AutoLift_1_Direction = -1 *
                            AutoLift_1_Direction;
    }
}
```

Script 작성 후에, 컴파일하고 저장한다 > Visual Studio를 종료한다 > Unity Editor로 온다. 왼쪽 Hierarchy에서 Player 선택 > 오른쪽 Inspector > Player Controller (Script) 아래를 보면 AutoLift_1 옆이 None (GameObject)로 되어 있다 > 왼쪽 Hierarchy에서 AutoLift_1를 click & drag 형태로 끌어다가 이 빈칸에 넣는다.

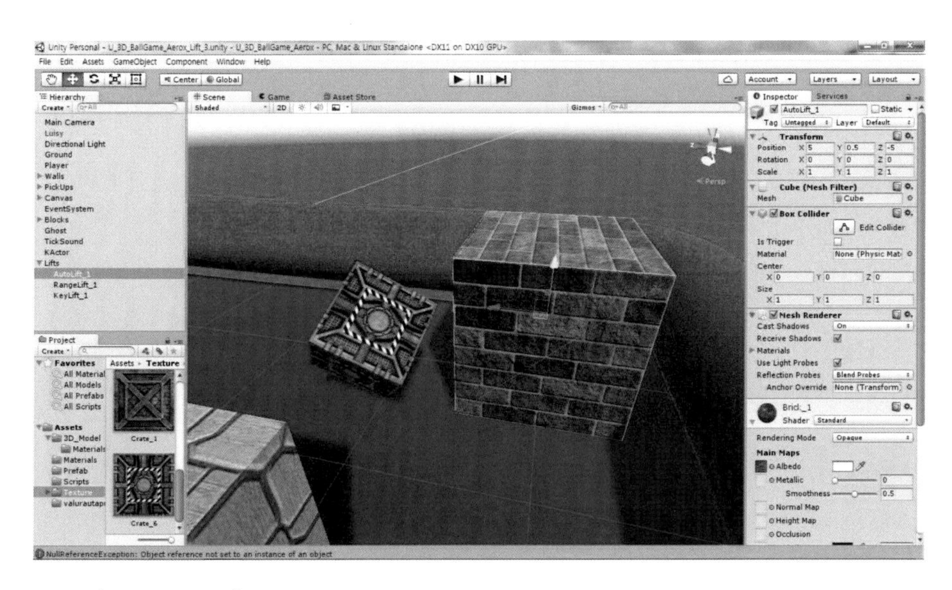

Fig 6. Auto Lift

33. 일정한 반경 안에 들어와 있는 경우, 반복적으로 움직이는 Range Lift 만드는 법

Range Lift는 Ball player와의 거리가 중요하다. 그런데 위/아래로 움직인다고 해서 RigidBody 형태가 아니다. 단순히 기본적인 GameObject Cube 형태이다.

메뉴 Game Object 〉 3D Object 〉 Cube 선택한다 〉 이름을 RangeLift_1로 수정한다 〉 RangeLift_1를 집어다가 Lifts 아래로 넣는다 〉 오른쪽 Inspector 〉 Transform rollout 〉 5, 0.5, 0, 0, 0, 0, 1, 1, 1로 수정한다 〉 원하는 texture를 입힌다.

Ball player가 일정한 반경 안에 들어와 있는 경우에만 RangeLift_1가 자동으로 움직이도록 Script를 작성하기 위해서, Project 〉 Assets folder 〉 Scripts folder 〉 PlayerController를 double click 〉 그러면 Visual Studio가 실행된다 〉 아래 script를 작성한다. 참고로, PlayerController에다 script를 작성하는 이유는 RangeLift는 ball player와의 거리에 상관하기 때문이다.

```
<Script #13>
using UnityEngine;
using UnityEngine.UI;        //5  Header file for text on screen
using System.Collections;

public class PlayerController : MonoBehaviour {
    const int UP = 1;                    //13  UP direction
    const int DOWN = -1;                 //13  DOWN direction

    public float speed = 10.0f;     //1  moving speed of ball
    public Text CountText;    //5  text on screen to show score
    public Text GameOverText;
            //6  text on screen to show "Game Over" message
    public Text TimerText;    //7  text on screen to show timer
    public AudioSource TickSound;
            //9  wave file to make sound

    public GameObject AutoLift_1;
                    //12  Auto Lift #1 at the right front corner
```

```
public GameObject RangeLift_1;
        //13  Range Lift #1 at the right middle corner
private Rigidbody rb;              //1  ball itself
private float MoveHorizontal;
                    //1  horizontal movement of ball
private float MoveVertical;    //1  vertical movement of ball
private Vector3 movement;   //1  final movement of ball
private int count;         //5  number of pickup items that
                    //      the ball has collected
private int NumberOfPickUps = 12;
                    //6  number of pickup items
private float StartTime;                 //7  starting time
private bool GameHasFinished = false
              //7  condition if game has finished or not
private float ElapsedTime;
        //7  elapsed time = current time - start time
private string Minutes;       //7  minutes
private string Seconds;       //7  seconds
private bool held_Q;  //10  input key 'Q' to make ball stop

private int AutoLift_1_Direction = DOWN;
        //12  initial direction of AutoLift_1 is down, where
        //       1 = up and -1 = down
private float AutoLift_1_BottomLimit = -0.4f;
        //12  bottom limit of movement of AutoLift_1
```

```
private float AutoLift_1_TopLimit = 0.5f;
        //12  top limit of movement of AutoLift_1

private int RangeLift_1_Direction = DOWN;
        //13  initial direction of RangeLift_1 is down,
        //       where 1 = up and -1 = down
private float RangeLift_1_BottomLimit = -0.4f;
        //13  bottom limit of movement of RangeLift_1
private float RangeLift_1_TopLimit = 0.5f;
        //13  top limit of movement of RangeLift_1
private float RangeLift_1_Collision_radius = 1.3f;
        //13  collision radius of RangeLift_1,
        //       where 1.3 = 0.5 (for ball radius)
        //       + 0.707 (for cube diagonal radius)
private float distance_of_RangeLift_1;
        //13  distance between the ball player and
        //       range lift_1
private float distance_X_of_RangeLift_1;
        //13  distance in X direction between
        //       the ball player and range lift_1
private float distance_Z_of_RangeLift_1;
        //13  distance in Z direction between the
        //       ball player and range lift_1

//9  Make a wave file ready to play
```

```
void Awake()  //9  Make a wave file ready to play
{
    if (TickSound == null)
          //9  if TickSound file is not ready to play,
    {
        TickSound = GameObject.Find("TickSound").
         GetComponent<AudioSource>();
          //9  find it in Hierarchy and make it ready to play
    }
}

// Use this for initialization
void Start () {
    rb = GetComponent<Rigidbody>();  //1  ball itself

    count = 0;  //5  initial value
    CountText.text = "Count: " + count.ToString();
                                   //5  show count on screen

    GameOverText.text = ""  //6  message "Game Over !!!"
    StartTime = Time.time;            //7  starting time
    TimerText.color = Color.yellow;
                          //7  set timer color to yellow
}
```

```
// Update is called once per frame
void FixedUpdate () {  //1 FixedUpdate() instead of Update()
    // Get key inputs to make ball roll around
    MoveHorizontal = Input.GetAxis("Horizontal");
                        //1  horizontal movement of ball
    MoveVertical = Input.GetAxis("Vertical");
                        //1  vertical movement of ball

    movement = new Vector3(MoveHorizontal, 0.0f,
                MoveVertical);  //1  final movement of ball
    rb.AddForce(movement * speed);
                //1  modify direction of ball movement

    if (GameHasFinished == false)
        //7  while ball is collecting 12 pickup items,
    {
        ElapsedTime = Time.time - StartTime;
         //7  elapsed time = current time - start time
        Minutes = ((int)ElapsedTime / 60).ToString();
        Seconds = (ElapsedTime % 60).ToString("f0");
         //7  "f0" means integer value format for seconds,
         //       not float value format
        TimerText.text = "Elapsed Time: " + Minutes + "M "
         + Seconds + "S";
                        //7  show elapsed time on screen
```

```
    }

    //10 Press 'Q' key to make the ball player stop
    held_Q = Input.GetKey(KeyCode.Q);  //10
    if (held_Q == true) rb.velocity = Vector3.zero;
                 //10  If 'Q key pressed, make the ball stop

    //  12, 13    C A L L     M A T I N E E
    UF_MATINEE();  //12, 13  call UF_MATINEE() for all lifts
}

//4 When collision happens with other, it is called
void OnTriggerEnter(Collider Other) {
  //4  When ball hits something, this function is called
    //4  If ball player hits something with tag = "PickUp",
    if (Other.gameObject .CompareTag("PickUp")) {
        Other.gameObject.SetActive(false);  //4  hide it

        count = count + 1;  //5  increase count by 1
        CountText.text = "Count: " + count.ToString();
                                   //5  update count on screen
        TickSound.Play();          //9  play TickSound file
                 //       when ball player hits a pickup item
    }
    if (count == NumberOfPickUps)
```

```
        //6  If ball player has collected 12 pickup items,
    {
        GameOverText.text = "Game Over !!!"
                //6  set GameOverText = "Game Over !!!"

        GameHasFinished = true
                //7  Game has finished because the ball
                //       has collected all 12 pickup items
        TimerText.color = Color.red;
                //7  change timer color to red
    }
}

//  12, 13    M A T I N E E
void UF_MATINEE()
{
    //12  AutoLift_1 - automatic lift moving up and down
    //    in the range of [AutoLift_1_BottomLimit ..
    //    AutoLift_1_TopLimit]
    if ((AutoLift_1_Direction == UP) &&
        (AutoLift_1.transform.position.y <
                AutoLift_1_TopLimit))
                AutoLift_1.transform.position =
                AutoLift_1.transform.position +
                    new Vector3(0.0f, 0.01f, 0.0f);
```

```
if ((AutoLift_1_Direction == UP) &&
      (AutoLift_1.transform.position.y >=
            AutoLift_1_TopLimit))
            AutoLift_1_Direction = -1 *
                  AutoLift_1_Direction;

if ((AutoLift_1_Direction == DOWN) &&
      (AutoLift_1.transform.position.y >
            AutoLift_1_BottomLimit))
            AutoLift_1.transform.position =
                  AutoLift_1.transform.position +
                  new Vector3(0.0f, -0.01f, 0.0f);

if ((AutoLift_1_Direction == DOWN) &&
      (AutoLift_1.transform.position.y <=
            AutoLift_1_BottomLimit))
            AutoLift_1_Direction = -1 *
                  AutoLift_1_Direction;

//13 RangeLift_1 - range lift moving up and down
//    in the range of [RangeLift_1_BottomLimit ..
//    RangeLift_1_TopLimit]
//    when ball player is near the range lift
distance_X_of_RangeLift_1 = rb.transform.position.x -
      RangeLift_1.transform.position.x;
```

```
                                //13  distance in X direction
distance_Z_of_RangeLift_1 = rb.transform.position.z -
    RangeLift_1.transform.position.z;
                                //13  distance in Z direction

distance_of_RangeLift_1 =
    Mathf.Sqrt((distance_X_of_RangeLift_1 *
                distance_X_of_RangeLift_1) +
                (distance_Z_of_RangeLift_1 *
                distance_Z_of_RangeLift_1));

if (distance_of_RangeLift_1 <=
    RangeLift_1_Collision_radius)
    //13  if ball player is in the collision radius,
{
   if ((RangeLift_1_Direction == UP) &&
    (RangeLift_1.transform.position.y <
          RangeLift_1_TopLimit))
          RangeLift_1.transform.position =
                RangeLift_1.transform.position +
                new Vector3(0.0f, 0.01f, 0.0f);

   if ((RangeLift_1_Direction == UP) &&
    (RangeLift_1.transform.position.y >=
          RangeLift_1_TopLimit))
```

```
                    RangeLift_1_Direction = -1 *
                            RangeLift_1_Direction;

            if ((RangeLift_1_Direction == DOWN) &&
             (RangeLift_1.transform.position.y >
                    RangeLift_1_BottomLimit))
                    RangeLift_1.transform.position =
                            RangeLift_1.transform.position +
                            new Vector3(0.0f, -0.01f, 0.0f);

            if ((RangeLift_1_Direction == DOWN) &&
             (RangeLift_1.transform.position.y <=
                    RangeLift_1_BottomLimit))
                    RangeLift_1_Direction = -1 *
                            RangeLift_1_Direction;
        }
    }
}
```

Script 작성 후에, 컴파일하고 저장한다 〉 Visual Studio를 종료한다 〉 Unity Editor로 온다. 왼쪽 Hierarchy에서 Player 선택 〉 오른쪽 Inspector 〉 Player Controller (Script) 아래를 보면 RangeLift_1 옆이 None (GameObject)로 되어 있다 〉 왼쪽 Hierarchy에서 RangeLift_1를 click & drag 형태로 끌어다가 이 빈칸에 넣는다.

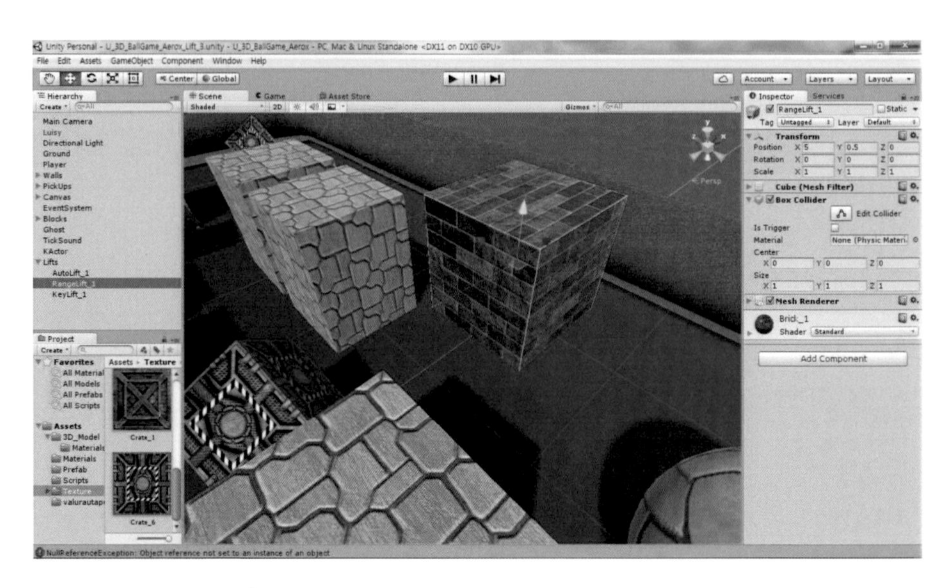

Fig 7. Range Lift

34. 일정한 반경 안에 들어와 있는 경우, Key값으로 움직이는 Key Lift 만드는 법

참고로, Key Lift는 Ball player와의 거리와 키값이 중요하다. 그런데 위/아래로 움직인다고 해서 RigidBody 형태가 아니다. 단순히 기본적인 GameObject Cube 형태이다.

메뉴 Game Object 〉 3D Object 〉 Cube 선택한다 〉 이름을 KeyLift_1로 수정한다 〉 KeyLift_1를 집어다가 Lifts 아래로 넣는다 〉 오른쪽 Inspector 〉 Transform rollout 〉 -2, 0.5, -5, 0, 0, 0, 1, 1, 1로 수정한다 〉 원하는 texture를 입힌다.

Ball player가 일정한 반경 안에 들어와 있는 경우에만 KeyLift_1가 키

값을 받아 움직이도록 Script를 작성하기 위해서, Project 〉 Assets folder 〉 Scripts folder 〉 PlayerController를 double click 〉 그러면 Visual Studio가 실행된다 〉 아래 script를 작성한다.

〈Script #14〉

```
using UnityEngine;
using UnityEngine.UI;        //5  Header file for text on screen
using System.Collections;

public class PlayerController : MonoBehaviour {
    const int UP = 1;              //13  UP direction
    const int DOWN = -1;           //13  DOWN direction

    public float speed = 10.0f;        //1  moving speed of ball
    public Text CountText;    //5  text on screen to show score
    public Text GameOverText;
            //6  text on screen to show "Game Over" message
    public Text TimerText;    //7  text on screen to show timer
    public AudioSource TickSound;  //9  wave file to make
                //  sound when player hits a pickup item
    public GameObject AutoLift_1;
                //12  Auto Lift #1 at the right front corner
    public GameObject RangeLift_1;
            //13  Range Lift #1 at the right middle corner
    public GameObject KeyLift_1;
```

```
        //14  Key Lift #1 at the middle front corner

private Rigidbody rb;            //1  ball itself
private float MoveHorizontal;
                        //1  horizontal movement of ball
private float MoveVertical;     //1  vertical movement of ball
private Vector3 movement;   //1  final movement of ball
private int count;
  //5  number of pickup items that the ball has collected
private int NumberOfPickUps = 12;
                              //6  number of pickup items
private float StartTime;                  //7  starting time
private bool GameHasFinished = false;
                //7  condition if game has finished or not
private float ElapsedTime;
        //7  elapsed time = current time - start time
private string Minutes;       //7  minutes
private string Seconds;       //7  seconds
private bool held_Q = false;    //10  input key 'Q' to make
                              //       ball stop

private int AutoLift_1_Direction = DOWN;
                //12  initial direction of AutoLift_1 is
                //       down, where 1 = up and -1 = down
private float AutoLift_1_BottomLimit = -0.4f;
```

```
            //12  bottom limit of movement of AutoLift_1
private float AutoLift_1_TopLimit = 0.5f;
            //12  top limit of movement of AutoLift_1

private int RangeLift_1_Direction = DOWN;
            //13  initial direction of RangeLift_1 is down,
            //      where 1 = up and -1 = down
private float RangeLift_1_BottomLimit = -0.4f;
            //13  bottom limit of movement of RangeLift_1
private float RangeLift_1_TopLimit = 0.5f;
            //13  top limit of movement of RangeLift_1
private float RangeLift_1_Collision_radius = 1.3f;
            //13  collision radius of RangeLift_1,
            //      where 1.3 = 0.5 (for ball radius) +
            //      0.707 (for cube diagonal radius)
private float distance_of_RangeLift_1;
            //13  distance between the ball player and
            //      RangeLift_1
private float distance_X_of_RangeLift_1;
            //13  distance in X direction between the ball
            //      player and RangeLift_1
private float distance_Z_of_RangeLift_1;
            //13  distance in Z direction between the ball
            //      player and RangeLift_1
```

```
private float KeyLift_1_BottomLimit = -0.4f;
        //14  bottom limit of movement of KeyLift_1
private float KeyLift_1_TopLimit = 0.5f;
        //14  top limit of movement of KeyLift_1
private float KeyLift_1_Collision_radius = 1.3f;
        //14  collision radius of KeyLift_1,
        //      where 1.3 = 0.5 (for ball radius) +
        //      0.707 (for cube diagonal radius)
private float distance_of_KeyLift_1;
        //14  distance between the ball player and
        //      KeyLift_1
private float distance_X_of_KeyLift_1;
        //14  distance in X direction between the ball
        //      player and KeyLift_1
private float distance_Z_of_KeyLift_1;
        //14  distance in Z direction between the ball
        //      player and KeyLift_1
private bool held_R = false;
        //14  input key 'R' to make lift go up
private bool held_F = false;
        //14  input key 'F' to make lift go down

//9  Make a wave file ready to play
void Awake()  //9  Make a wave file ready to play
{
```

```
    if (TickSound == null)
        //9  if TickSound file is not ready to play,
    {
        TickSound = GameObject.Find("TickSound").
         GetComponent<AudioSource>();
         //9  find it in Hierarchy and make it ready to play
    }
}

// Use this for initialization
void Start () {
    rb = GetComponent<Rigidbody>();  //1  ball itself

    count = 0;  //5  initial value
    CountText.text = "Count: " + count.ToString();
                                   //5  show count on screen

    GameOverText.text = "";  //6  message "Game Over !!!"
    StartTime = Time.time;             //7  starting time
    TimerText.color = Color.yellow;
  }

  // Update is called once per frame
  void FixedUpdate () {
    // Get key inputs to make ball roll around
```

```
MoveHorizontal = Input.GetAxis("Horizontal");
                    //1  horizontal movement of ball
MoveVertical = Input.GetAxis("Vertical");
                    //1  vertical movement of ball

movement = new Vector3(MoveHorizontal, 0.0f,
            MoveVertical);  //1  final movement of ball
rb.AddForce(movement * speed);
            //1  modify direction of ball movement

if (GameHasFinished == false)   //7  while ball is
                    //      collecting 12 pickup items,
{
    ElapsedTime = Time.time - StartTime;
     //7  elapsed time = current time - start time
    Minutes = ((int)ElapsedTime / 60).ToString();
    Seconds = (ElapsedTime % 60).ToString("f0");
    TimerText.text = "Elapsed Time: " + Minutes + "M "
                    + Seconds + "S";
                    //7  show elapsed time on screen
}

//10 Press 'Q' key to make the ball player stop
held_Q = Input.GetKey(KeyCode.Q);  //10
if (held_Q == true) rb.velocity = Vector3.zero;
```

```
            //10  If 'Q key pressed, make the ball stop

    //  12, 13, 14       C A L L     M A T I N E E
    UF_MATINEE();  //12-14  call UF_MATINEE() for all lifts
  }

//4 When collision happens with other, it is called
void OnTriggerEnter(Collider Other) {
  //4  When ball hits something, this function is called

    //4  If ball player hits something with tag = "PickUp",
    if (Other.gameObject .CompareTag("PickUp")) {
        Other.gameObject.SetActive(false);        //4  hide it
        count = count + 1;  //5  increase count by 1
        CountText.text = "Count: " + count.ToString();
                                 //5  update count on screen
        TickSound.Play();  //9  play TickSound file when
                          //      ball player hits a pickup item
    }

    if (count == NumberOfPickUps)
          //6  If ball player has collected 12 pickup items,
    {
        GameOverText.text = "Game Over !!!";
                //6  set GameOverText = "Game Over !!!"
```

```
        GameHasFinished = true;
                //7  Game has finished because the ball
                //      has collected all 12 pickup items
        TimerText.color = Color.red;
                    //7  change timer color to red
    }
}

// 12, 13, 14       M A T I N E E
void UF_MATINEE() {

    //12  AutoLift_1 - automatic lift moving up and down
  //      in the range of [AutoLift_1_BottomLimit ..
  //      AutoLift_1_TopLimit]
    if ((AutoLift_1_Direction == UP) &&
        (AutoLift_1.transform.position.y <
            AutoLift_1_TopLimit))
            AutoLift_1.transform.position =
                AutoLift_1.transform.position +
                new Vector3(0.0f, 0.01f, 0.0f);

    if ((AutoLift_1_Direction == UP) &&
        (AutoLift_1.transform.position.y >=
            AutoLift_1_TopLimit))
            AutoLift_1_Direction = -1 *
```

```
                    AutoLift_1_Direction;

if ((AutoLift_1_Direction == DOWN) &&
    (AutoLift_1.transform.position.y >
          AutoLift_1_BottomLimit))
          AutoLift_1.transform.position =
                    AutoLift_1.transform.position +
                    new Vector3(0.0f, -0.01f, 0.0f);

if ((AutoLift_1_Direction == DOWN) &&
    (AutoLift_1.transform.position.y <=
          AutoLift_1_BottomLimit))
          AutoLift_1_Direction = -1 *
                    AutoLift_1_Direction;

//13 RangeLift_1 - range lift moving up and down in
//    the range of [RangeLift_1_BottomLimit ..
//    RangeLift_1_TopLimit]

// when ball player is near the range lift
distance_X_of_RangeLift_1 = rb.transform.position.x -
    RangeLift_1.transform.position.x;
                              //13  distance in X direction
distance_Z_of_RangeLift_1 = rb.transform.position.z -
    RangeLift_1.transform.position.z;
```

```
                              //13  distance in Z direction
distance_of_RangeLift_1 =
    Mathf.Sqrt((distance_X_of_RangeLift_1 *
                    distance_X_of_RangeLift_1) +
                    (distance_Z_of_RangeLift_1 *
                    distance_Z_of_RangeLift_1));
                              //  13  distance

if (distance_of_RangeLift_1 <=
    RangeLift_1_Collision_radius)
    //13  if ball player is in the collision radius,
{
   if ((RangeLift_1_Direction == UP) &&
         (RangeLift_1.transform.position.y <
         RangeLift_1_TopLimit))
         RangeLift_1.transform.position =
               RangeLift_1.transform.position +
               new Vector3(0.0f, 0.01f, 0.0f);

   if ((RangeLift_1_Direction == UP) &&
         (RangeLift_1.transform.position.y >=
         RangeLift_1_TopLimit))
         RangeLift_1_Direction = -1 *
               RangeLift_1_Direction;
```

```
    if ((RangeLift_1_Direction == DOWN) &&
            (RangeLift_1.transform.position.y >
            RangeLift_1_BottomLimit))
            RangeLift_1.transform.position =
                    RangeLift_1.transform.position +
                    new Vector3(0.0f, -0.01f, 0.0f);

    if ((RangeLift_1_Direction == DOWN) &&
            (RangeLift_1.transform.position.y <=
            RangeLift_1_BottomLimit))
            RangeLift_1_Direction = -1 *
                    RangeLift_1_Direction;
}

//14 KeyLift_1 - key lift moving up and down in the
//    range of [RangeLift_1_BottomLimit ..
//    RangeLift_1_TopLimit]

// when ball player is near the range lift,  and also
// 'R' or 'F' key is pressed
distance_X_of_KeyLift_1 = rb.transform.position.x -
                    KeyLift_1.transform.position.x;
                            //14  distance in X direction
distance_Z_of_KeyLift_1 = rb.transform.position.z -
                    KeyLift_1.transform.position.z;
```

```
                                  //14  distance in Z direction

distance_of_KeyLift_1 =
    Mathf.Sqrt((distance_X_of_KeyLift_1 *
    distance_X_of_KeyLift_1) + (distance_Z_of_KeyLift_1
    * distance_Z_of_KeyLift_1));            //14  distance

if (distance_of_KeyLift_1 <= KeyLift_1_Collision_radius)
    //14  if ball player is in the collision radius,
{
   held_R = Input.GetKey(KeyCode.R);
                  //14  check if 'R' key is pressed
   held_F = Input.GetKey(KeyCode.F);
                  //14  check if 'F' key is pressed

   if ((held_R == true) &&
          (KeyLift_1.transform.position.y <
          KeyLift_1_TopLimit))
          KeyLift_1.transform.position =
                KeyLift_1.transform.position +
                      new Vector3(0.0f, 0.01f, 0.0f);

   if ((held_F == true) &&
          (KeyLift_1.transform.position.y >
          KeyLift_1_BottomLimit))
```

```
                KeyLift_1.transform.position =
                    KeyLift_1.transform.position +
                    new Vector3(0.0f, -0.01f, 0.0f);
        }
    }
}
```

Script 작성 후에, 컴파일하고 저장한다 〉 Visual Studio를 종료한다 〉 Unity Editor로 온다. 왼쪽 Hierarchy에서 Player 선택 〉 오른쪽 Inspector 〉 Player Controller (Script) 아래를 보면 KeyLift_1 옆이 None (GameObject)로 되어 있다 〉 왼쪽 Hierarchy에서 KeyLift_1를 click & drag 형태로 끌어다가 이 빈칸에 넣는다.

35. 일정한 반경 안에 들어와 있는 경우, 자동으로 위로 점프하는 Jump Pad 만드는 법

Ball player가 Jump Pad 위로 올라오면 자동으로 점프한다. 단순히 기본적인 GameObject Cube 형태이다. 메뉴 Game Object 〉 3D Object 〉 Cube 선택한다 〉 이름을 JumpPad_1로 수정한다 〉 오른쪽 Inspector 〉 Transform rollout 〉 0, -0.45, -3, 0, 0, 0, 1, 1, 1로 수정한다 〉 원하는 texture를 입힌다. Ball player가 Jump Pad 위로 올라오면 자동으로 점프하도록 Script를 작성하기 위해서, Project 〉 Assets folder 〉 Scripts folder 〉 PlayerController를 double click 〉 그러면 Visual Studio가 실행된다 〉 아래 script를 작성한다.

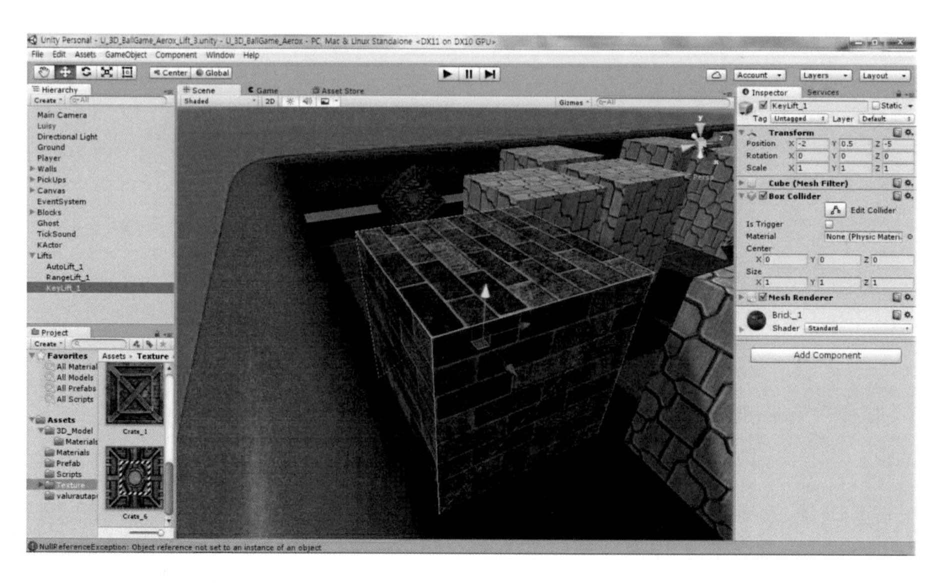

Fig 8. Key Lift

〈Script #15〉

```
using System.Collections;
using System.Collections.Generic;
using UnityEngine;
using UnityEngine.UI;           //5  Header file for text on screen

public class PlayerController : MonoBehaviour {
    const int UP = 1;                //13  UP direction
    const int DOWN = -1;             //13  DOWN direction

    public float speed = 10.0f;      //1  moving speed of ball
```

```
public Text CountText;   //5  text on screen to show score
public Text GameOverText;
         //6  text on screen to show "Game Over" message
public Text TimerText;   //7  text on screen to show timer

public AudioSource TickSound;   //9  wave file to make
                  // sound when player hits a pickup item

public GameObject AutoLift_1;
                  //12  Auto Lift #1 at the right front corner
public GameObject RangeLift_1;
         //13  Range Lift #1 at the right middle corner
public GameObject KeyLift_1;
         //14  Key Lift #1 at the middle front corner
public GameObject JumpPad_1;   //15  Jump Pad #1
private Rigidbody rb;          //1  ball itself
private float MoveHorizontal;
                          //1  horizontal movement of ball
private float MoveVertical;
                          //1  vertical movement of ball
private Vector3 movement;      //1  final movement of ball

private int count;        //5  number of pickup items that
                          //     the ball has collected
```

```
private int NumberOfPickUps = 12;
                                    //6  number of pickup items
private float StartTime;                   //7  starting time
private bool GameHasFinished = false;
                  //7  condition if game has finished or not
private float ElapsedTime;
          //7  elapsed time = current time - start time
private string Minutes;                    //7  minutes
private string Seconds;                    //7  seconds

private bool held_Q = false;    //10  input key 'Q' to make
                                //       ball stop
private int AutoLift_1_Direction = DOWN;
          //12  initial direction of AutoLift_1 is down,
          //       where 1 = up and -1 = down
private float AutoLift_1_BottomLimit = -0.4f;
          //12  bottom limit of movement of AutoLift_1
private float AutoLift_1_TopLimit = 0.5f;
          //12  top limit of movement of AutoLift_1

private int RangeLift_1_Direction = DOWN;
          //13  initial direction of RangeLift_1 is down,
          //       where 1 = up and -1 = down
private float RangeLift_1_BottomLimit = -0.4f;
          //13  bottom limit of movement of RangeLift_1
```

```
private float RangeLift_1_TopLimit = 0.5f;
        //13  top limit of movement of RangeLift_1
private float RangeLift_1_Collision_radius = 1.3f;
        //13  collision radius of RangeLift_1,
        //      where 1.3 = 0.5 (for ball radius) +
        //      0.707 (for cube diagonal radius)
private float distance_of_RangeLift_1;
        //13  distance between the ball player
        //      and RangeLift_1
private float distance_X_of_RangeLift_1;
        //13  distance in X direction between the ball
        //      player and RangeLift_1
private float distance_Z_of_RangeLift_1;
        //13  distance in Z direction between the ball
        //      player and RangeLift_1

private float KeyLift_1_BottomLimit = -0.4f;
        //14  bottom limit of movement of KeyLift_1
private float KeyLift_1_TopLimit = 0.5f;
        //14  top limit of movement of KeyLift_1
private float KeyLift_1_Collision_radius = 1.3f;
        //14  collision radius of KeyLift_1,
        //      where 1.3 = 0.5 (for ball radius) +
        //      0.707 (for cube diagonal radius)
private float distance_of_KeyLift_1;
```

```
  //14  distance between the ball player and KeyLift_1
private float distance_X_of_KeyLift_1;
  //14  distance in X direction between the ball player
  //      and KeyLift_1
private float distance_Z_of_KeyLift_1;
  //14  distance in Z direction between the ball player
  //      and KeyLift_1
private bool held_R = false;
                    //14  input key 'R' to make lift go up
private bool held_F = false;
                    //14  input key 'F' to make lift go down

private float JumpPad_1_Collision_radius = 0.5f;
                    //15  collision radius of JumpPad_1
private float distance_of_JumpPad_1;
  //15  distance between the ball player and JumpPad_1
private float distance_X_of_JumpPad_1;
  //15  distance in X direction between the ball player
  //      and JumpPad_1
private float distance_Z_of_JumpPad_1;
  //15  distance in Z direction between the ball player
  //      and JumpPad_1

//9  Make a wave file ready to play
void Awake() {  //9  Make a wave file ready to play
```

```
        if (TickSound == null) {//9  if TickSound file is not
                                //      ready to play,

        TickSound = GameObject.Find("TickSound").
                        GetComponent<AudioSource>();
         //9  find it in Hierarchy and make it ready to play
    }
}

// Use this for initialization
void Start () {
    rb = GetComponent<Rigidbody>();  //1  ball itself
    count = 0;  //5  initial value
    CountText.text = "Count: " + count.ToString();
                                //5  show count on screen
    GameOverText.text = "";     //6  message "Game Over !!!"

    StartTime = Time.time;              //7  starting time
    TimerText.color = Color.yellow;
                        //7  set timer color to yellow
}

// Update is called once per frame
void FixedUpdate() {  //1 FixedUpdate() instead of Update()
```

```
// Get key inputs to make ball roll around
MoveHorizontal = Input.GetAxis("Horizontal");
                    //1  horizontal movement of ball
MoveVertical = Input.GetAxis("Vertical");
                    //1  vertical movement of ball

movement = new Vector3(MoveHorizontal, 0.0f,
            MoveVertical);  //1  final movement of ball
rb.AddForce(movement * speed);
            //1  modify direction of ball movement

if (GameHasFinished == false) {   //7  while ball is
                    // collecting 12 pickup items,
    ElapsedTime = Time.time - StartTime;
     //7  elapsed time = current time - start time
    Minutes = ((int)ElapsedTime / 60).ToString();
    Seconds = (ElapsedTime % 60).ToString("f0");
    TimerText.text = "Elapsed Time: " + Minutes + "M "
                    + Seconds + "S";
                    //7  show elapsed time on screen
}

//10 Press 'Q' key to make the ball player stop
held_Q = Input.GetKey(KeyCode.Q);
if (held_Q == true) rb.velocity = Vector3.zero;
```

```
                //10  If 'Q key pressed, make the ball stop

    //  12, 13, 14, 15      C A L L     M A T I N E E
    UF_MATINEE();  // call for all lifts and jump pad
}

//4 When collision happens with other, it is called
void OnTriggerEnter(Collider Other) {
  //4  When ball hits something, this function is called

    //4  If ball player hits something with tag = "PickUp",
    if (Other.gameObject.CompareTag("PickUp")) {
        Other.gameObject.SetActive(false);        //4  hide it

        count = count + 1;  //5  increase count by 1
        CountText.text = "Count: " + count.ToString();
                                   //5  update count on screen

        TickSound.Play();  //9  play TickSound file when
                         //  ball player hits a pickup item
    }

    if (count == NumberOfPickUps) {
         //6  If ball player has collected 12 pickup items,
        GameOverText.text = "GAME OVER";
```

```
            //6  set GameOverText = "Game Over !!!"

        GameHasFinished = true;   //7  Game has finished
         //because the ball has collected 12 pickup items
        TimerText.color = Color.red;
                          //7  change timer color to red
    }
}

// 12, 13, 14, 15      M A T I N E E
void UF_MATINEE() {

    //12  AutoLift_1 - automatic lift moving up and down
    //    in the range of [AutoLift_1_BottomLimit ..
    //    AutoLift_1_TopLimit]
    if ((AutoLift_1_Direction == UP) &&
         (AutoLift_1.transform.position.y <
              AutoLift_1_TopLimit))
              AutoLift_1.transform.position =
                   AutoLift_1.transform.position +
                   new Vector3(0.0f, 0.01f, 0.0f);

    if ((AutoLift_1_Direction == UP) &&
         (AutoLift_1.transform.position.y >=
              AutoLift_1_TopLimit))
```

```
            AutoLift_1_Direction = -1 *
                    AutoLift_1_Direction;

if ((AutoLift_1_Direction == DOWN) &&
    (AutoLift_1.transform.position.y >
            AutoLift_1_BottomLimit))
            AutoLift_1.transform.position =
                    AutoLift_1.transform.position +
                    new Vector3(0.0f, -0.01f, 0.0f);

if ((AutoLift_1_Direction == DOWN) &&
    (AutoLift_1.transform.position.y <=
            AutoLift_1_BottomLimit))
            AutoLift_1_Direction = -1 *
                    AutoLift_1_Direction;

//13 RangeLift_1 - range lift moving up and down in
//    the range of [RangeLift_1_BottomLimit ..
//    RangeLift_1_TopLimit]
// when ball player is near the range lift
distance_X_of_RangeLift_1 = rb.transform.position.x -
    RangeLift_1.transform.position.x;
                              //13  distance in X direction
distance_Z_of_RangeLift_1 = rb.transform.position.z -
    RangeLift_1.transform.position.z;
```

```
                              //13  distance in Z direction

distance_of_RangeLift_1 =
    Mathf.Sqrt((distance_X_of_RangeLift_1 *
    distance_X_of_RangeLift_1) +
    (distance_Z_of_RangeLift_1 *
    distance_Z_of_RangeLift_1));  //  13  distance

if (distance_of_RangeLift_1 <=
    RangeLift_1_Collision_radius)
    //13  if ball player is in the collision radius,
{
   if ((RangeLift_1_Direction == UP) &&
          (RangeLift_1.transform.position.y <
          RangeLift_1_TopLimit))
          RangeLift_1.transform.position =
                 RangeLift_1.transform.position +
                        new Vector3(0.0f, 0.01f, 0.0f);

   if ((RangeLift_1_Direction == UP) &&
          (RangeLift_1.transform.position.y >=
                 RangeLift_1_TopLimit))
                 RangeLift_1_Direction = -1 *
                        RangeLift_1_Direction;
```

```
    if ((RangeLift_1_Direction == DOWN) &&
            (RangeLift_1.transform.position.y >
                    RangeLift_1_BottomLimit))
                    RangeLift_1.transform.position =
                    RangeLift_1.transform.position +
                    new Vector3(0.0f, -0.01f, 0.0f);

    if ((RangeLift_1_Direction == DOWN) &&
            (RangeLift_1.transform.position.y <=
                    RangeLift_1_BottomLimit))
                    RangeLift_1_Direction = -1 *
                            RangeLift_1_Direction;
}

//14 KeyLift_1 - key lift moving up and down in the
//    range of [RangeLift_1_BottomLimit ..
//    RangeLift_1_TopLimit]
//     when ball player is near the range lift  and also
//    'R' or 'F' key is pressed
distance_X_of_KeyLift_1 = rb.transform.position.x -
      KeyLift_1.transform.position.x;
                               //14  distance in X direction
distance_Z_of_KeyLift_1 = rb.transform.position.z -
      KeyLift_1.transform.position.z;
                               //14  distance in Z direction
```

```
distance_of_KeyLift_1 =
      Mathf.Sqrt((distance_X_of_KeyLift_1 *
              distance_X_of_KeyLift_1) +
              (distance_Z_of_KeyLift_1 *
              distance_Z_of_KeyLift_1));  //  14  distance

if (distance_of_KeyLift_1 <= KeyLift_1_Collision_radius)
      //14  if ball player is in the collision radius,
{
    held_R = Input.GetKey(KeyCode.R);
                    //14  check if 'R' key is pressed
    held_F = Input.GetKey(KeyCode.F);
                    //14  check if 'F' key is pressed
    if ((held_R == true) &&
     (KeyLift_1.transform.position.y <
              KeyLift_1_TopLimit))
              KeyLift_1.transform.position =
                    KeyLift_1.transform.position +
                          new Vector3(0.0f, 0.01f, 0.0f);

    if ((held_F == true) &&
     (KeyLift_1.transform.position.y >
              KeyLift_1_BottomLimit))
              KeyLift_1.transform.position =
                    KeyLift_1.transform.position +
```

```
                new Vector3(0.0f, -0.01f, 0.0f);
        }

        //15 JumpPad_1 - Jump Pad to make ball player fly
        //    when ball player is on the Jump pad
        distance_X_of_JumpPad_1 = rb.transform.position.x -
            JumpPad_1.transform.position.x;
                                //15  distance in X direction
        distance_Z_of_JumpPad_1 = rb.transform.position.z -
            JumpPad_1.transform.position.z;
                                //15  distance in Z direction
        distance_of_JumpPad_1 = Mathf.Sqrt(
            (distance_X_of_JumpPad_1 *
            distance_X_of_JumpPad_1) +
            (distance_Z_of_JumpPad_1 *
            distance_Z_of_JumpPad_1));          //15  distance

        if (distance_of_JumpPad_1 <=
            JumpPad_1_Collision_radius)
                    //15  if ball player is on the Jump pad,
        {
            rb.AddForce(new Vector3(0.0f, 20.0f, 0.0f));
        }
    }
}
```

Script 작성 후에, 컴파일하고 저장한다 〉 Visual Studio를 종료한다 〉 Unity Editor로 온다. 왼쪽 Hierarchy에서 Player 선택 〉 오른쪽 Inspector 〉 Player Controller (Script) 아래를 보면 Jump Pad_1 옆이 None (GameObject)로 되어 있다 〉 왼쪽 Hierarchy에서 JumpPad_1를 click & drag 형태로 끌어다가 이 빈칸에 넣는다.

36. 3DS model Luisy를 import하는 법

Unity에서 사용가능한 3D model 형식은 *.fbx, *.dae, *.3ds, *.obj 등이다.

Fig 9. 3D Model Luisy

메뉴 Assets 〉 Import New Asset 〉 Luisy.3ds를 import 한다 〉 그러면, 왼쪽 Project 〉 Assets 〉 아래에 추가된다 〉 왼쪽 Project 〉 Assets 위에서 RMB click 〉 Create 〉 Folder 선택한다 〉 이름을 3D_Model 로 수정한다 〉 Luisy.3ds를 3D_Model folder로 이동시킨다 〉 Luisy.3ds를 click & drag 형태로 Scene에다 추가시킨다 〉 Hierarchy 〉 이름을 Luisy로 수정한다 〉 Inspector 〉 Transform rollout 〉 아래 값들을 5.5, 1,

7, 0, 180, 0, 0.03, 0.03, 0.03 으로 한다.

메뉴 Assets 〉 Import New Asset 〉 LuisyD.jpg 를 import 한다 〉 LuisyD.jpg를 3D_Model folder로 이동시킨다 〉 LuisyD.jpg를 click & drag 형태로 끌어다가 Scene에 있는 Luisy에 입힌다. 참고로, 현재 Text를 보이기 위해 Canvas가 생성되어 있으니 그 뒤로 돌아가서 Luisy 위에다 LuisyD.jpg를 입혀야 한다.

37. 구름다리 만드는 방법

출렁거리는 구름다리를 만들려면 Hinge joint를 사용해야 한다. 먼저, 지금까지 만든 바닥과 4개의 빨간색 벽을 선택하고 복사 〉 왼쪽으로 상대적으로 -15만큼 이동시켜 새로운 공간을 만든다 〉 Ball Player와 Camera 위치도 -15로 수정한다.

구름다리 발판들을 담기 위해서, 메뉴 Game Object 〉 Create Empty 선택 〉 왼쪽 Hierarchy에 Game Object 추가된다 〉 Bridge로 수정한다 〉 Bridge 선택 〉 오른쪽 Inspector 〉 톱니바퀴 click 〉 Reset 선택한다.

1) 첫 번째 발판을 만들기 위해서, 메뉴 Game Object 〉 3D Object 〉 Cube 선택 〉 이름을 Hinge1로 수정하고 〉 Bridge 아래로 이동한다 〉 오른쪽 Inspector 〉 Transform 〉 -15, 5, -5.5, 0, 0, 0, 1, 0.05, 1 로 수정한다 〉 원하는 Texture를 입힌다. 참고로, Hinge1은 첫 번째 발판이므로 움직이지 않는다.

2) 두 번째 발판을 만들기 위해서, Hinge1 선택 〉 복사해서 추가한다 〉

이름을 Hinge2로 수정한다 〉 오른쪽 Inspector 〉 Transform 〉 -15, 5, -4.4, 0, 0, 0, 1, 0.05, 1 로 수정한다 〉 왼쪽 Hierarchy에서 Hinge2 선택 〉 오른쪽 Inspector 〉 Add Component 〉 Physics 〉 Rigid Body 선택 〉 Rigid body Component 추가한다 〉 Add Component 〉 Physics 〉 Hinge Joint 선택 〉 Hinge Joint Component 추가한다 〉 오른쪽 Inspector 〉 Hinge Joint 〉 Connected Body = None, Anchor = 0, 0, -0.5 (Hinge Joint의 위치임), Axis = 1, 0, 0 (Hinge Joint의 회전축임), Connected Anchor = -15, 5, -4.9 로 수정한다. 실행해보면 두 번째 발판이 덜렁거리지만 매달려 있다.

3) 세 번째 발판을 만들기 위해서, Hinge2 선택 〉 복사해서 추가한다 〉 이름을 Hinge3로 수정한다 〉 오른쪽 Inspector 〉 Transform 〉 -15, 5, -3.3, 0, 0, 0, 1, 0.05, 1 로 수정한다 〉 왼쪽 Hierarchy에서 Hinge3 선택 〉 오른쪽 Inspector 〉 Add Component 〉 Physics 〉 Rigid Body 선택 〉 Rigid body Component 추가한다 〉 Add Component 〉 Physics 〉 Hinge Joint 선택 〉 Hinge Joint Component 추가한다 〉 오른쪽 Inspector 〉 Hinge Joint 〉 Connected Body = 왼쪽 Hierarchy에서 Hinge2를 Click & Drag로 끌어다가 넣는다. Anchor = 0, 0, -0.5 (Hinge Joint의 위치임), Axis = 1, 0, 0 (Hinge Joint의 회전축임), Connected Anchor = 0, 0, 0.6 으로 수정한다.

4) 네 번째 발판을 만들기 위해서, Hinge2 선택 〉 복사해서 추가한다 〉 이름을 Hinge4로 수정한다 〉 오른쪽 Inspector 〉 Transform 〉 -15, 5, -2.2, 0, 0, 0, 1, 0.05, 1 로 수정한다 〉 왼쪽 Hierarchy에서 Hinge4 선택 〉 오른쪽 Inspector 〉 Add Component 〉 Physics 〉 Rigid Body

선택 〉 Rigid body Component 추가한다 〉 Add Component 〉 Physics 〉 Hinge Joint 선택 〉 Hinge Joint Component 추가한다 〉 오른쪽 Inspector 〉 Hinge Joint 〉 Connected Body = 왼쪽 Hierarchy에서 Hinge3를 Click & Drag로 끌어다가 넣는다. Anchor = 0, 0, -0.5 (Hinge 위치), Axis = 1, 0, 0 (Hinge 회전축), Connected Anchor = 0, 0, 0.6 으로 수정한다.

5) 다섯 번째 발판을 만들기 위해서, Hinge2 선택 〉 복사해서 추가한다 〉 이름을 Hinge5로 수정한다 〉 오른쪽 Inspector 〉 Transform 〉 -15, 5, -1.1, 0, 0, 0, 1, 0.05, 1 로 수정한다 〉 왼쪽 Hierarchy에서 Hinge5 선택 〉 오른쪽 Inspector 〉 Add Component 〉 Physics 〉 Rigid Body 선택 〉 Rigid body Component 추가한다 〉 Add Component 〉 Physics 〉 Hinge Joint 선택 〉 Hinge Joint Component 추가한다 〉 오른쪽 Inspector 〉 Hinge Joint 〉 Connected Body = 왼쪽 Hierarchy에서 Hinge4를 Click & Drag로 끌어다가 넣는다. Anchor = 0, 0, -0.5 (Hinge 위치), Axis = 1, 0, 0 (Hinge 회전축), Connected Anchor = 0, 0, 0.6 으로 수정한다.

6) 여섯 번째 발판을 만들기 위해서, Hinge2 선택 〉 복사해서 추가한다 〉 이름을 Hinge6로 수정한다 〉 오른쪽 Inspector 〉 Transform 〉 -15, 5, 0, 0, 0, 0, 1, 0.05, 1 로 수정한다 〉 왼쪽 Hierarchy에서 Hinge6 선택 〉 오른쪽 Inspector 〉 Add Component 〉 Physics 〉 Rigid Body 선택 〉 Rigid body Component 추가한다 〉 Add Component 〉 Physics 〉 Hinge Joint 선택 〉 Hinge Joint Component 추가한다 〉 오른쪽 Inspector 〉 Hinge Joint 〉 Connected Body = 왼쪽 Hierarchy에

서 Hinge5를 Click & Drag로 끌어다가 넣는다. Anchor = 0, 0, -0.5 (Hinge 위치), Axis = 1, 0, 0 (Hinge 회전축), Connected Anchor = 0, 0, 0.6 으로 수정한다.

7) 일곱 번째 발판을 만들기 위해서, Hinge2 선택 〉 복사해서 추가한다 〉 이름을 Hinge7로 수정한다 〉 오른쪽 Inspector 〉 Transform 〉 -15, 5, 1.1, 0, 0, 0, 1, 0.05, 1 로 수정한다 〉 왼쪽 Hierarchy에서 Hinge7 선택 〉 오른쪽 Inspector 〉 Add Component 〉 Physics 〉 Rigid Body 선택 〉 Rigid body Component 추가한다 〉 Add Component 〉 Physics 〉 Hinge Joint 선택 〉 Hinge Joint Component 추가한다 〉 오른쪽 Inspector 〉 Hinge Joint 〉 Connected Body = 왼쪽 Hierarchy에서 Hinge6를 Click & Drag로 끌어다가 넣는다. Anchor = 0, 0, -0.5 (Hinge Joint의 위치임), Axis = 1, 0, 0 (Hinge Joint의 회전축임), Connected Anchor = 0, 0, 0.6 으로 수정한다.

8) 여덟 번째 발판을 만들기 위해서, Hinge2 선택 〉 복사해서 추가한다 〉 이름을 Hinge8로 수정한다 〉 오른쪽 Inspector 〉 Transform 〉 -15, 5, 2.2, 0, 0, 0, 1, 0.05, 1 로 수정한다 〉 왼쪽 Hierarchy에서 Hinge8 선택 〉 오른쪽 Inspector 〉 Add Component 〉 Physics 〉 Rigid Body 선택 〉 Rigid body Component 추가한다 〉 Add Component 〉 Physics 〉 Hinge Joint 선택 〉 Hinge Joint Component 추가한다 〉 오른쪽 Inspector 〉 Hinge Joint 〉 Connected Body = 왼쪽 Hierarchy에서 Hinge7를 Click & Drag로 끌어다가 넣는다. Anchor = 0, 0, -0.5 (Hinge Joint의 위치임), Axis = 1, 0, 0 (Hinge Joint의 회전축임), Connected Anchor = 0, 0, 0.6 으로 수정한다.

9) 아홉 번째 발판은 Hinge Joint를 2개 사용해야 한다. 아홉 번째 발판을 만들기 위해서, Hinge2 선택 〉 복사해서 추가한다 〉 이름을 Hinge9로 수정한다 〉 오른쪽 Inspector 〉 Transform 〉 -15, 5, 3.3, 0, 0, 0, 1, 0.05, 1 로 수정한다 〉 왼쪽 Hierarchy에서 Hinge9 선택 〉 오른쪽 Inspector 〉 Add Component 〉 Physics 〉 Rigid Body 선택 〉 Rigid body Component 추가한다 〉 Add Component 〉 Physics 〉 Hinge Joint 선택 〉 Hinge Joint Component 추가한다 〉 오른쪽 Inspector 〉 Hinge Joint 〉 Connected Body = 왼쪽 Hierarchy에서 Hinge8를 Click & Drag로 끌어다가 넣는다 〉 Anchor = 0, 0, -0.5 (Hinge Joint의 위치임), Axis = 1, 0, 0 (Hinge Joint의 회전축임), Connected Anchor = 0, 0, 0.6 으로 수정한다.

Hinge Joint Component 하나 더 추가하기 위해서, Add Component 〉 Physics 〉 Hinge Joint 선택 〉 Hinge Joint Component 추가한다 〉 오른쪽 Inspector 〉 Hinge Joint 〉 Connected Body = None 그대로 둔다 〉 Anchor = 0, 0, 0.5 (Hinge Joint의 위치임), Axis = 1, 0, 0 (Hinge Joint의 회전축임), Connected Anchor = -15, 5, 3.8 으로 수정한다.

10) 열 번째 발판을 만들기 위해서, Hinge1 선택 〉 복사해서 추가한다 〉 이름을 Hinge10로 수정한다 〉 오른쪽 Inspector 〉 Transform 〉 -15, 5, 4.4, 0, 0, 0, 1, 0.05, 1 로 수정한다. 참고로, Hinge10은 Rigid body Component와 Hinge Joint 사용하지 않는다. Hinge10은 마지막 발판이므로 움직이지 않는다.

38. 3D model Pipe를 import하는 법

메뉴 Assets 〉 Import New Asset 〉 pipe 세 종류를 import 한다 〉 그러면, 왼쪽 Project 〉 Assets 〉 아래에 추가된다 〉 pipe 세 종류를 3D_Model folder로 이동시킨다 〉 Pipe_Bend_90을 click & drag 형태로 Scene에다 추가시킨다 〉 Hierarchy 〉 이름을 Pipe90으로 수정한다 〉 Inspector 〉 Transform rollout 〉 아래 값들을 -19, 0.7, 3, 0, 180, 0, 0.2, 0.2, 0.2 으로 한다. 참고로, 현재로서는 Collision이 설정되어 있지 않아서 충돌이 일어나지 않는다.

Collision을 설정하기 위해서, 왼쪽 Hierarchy 〉 Pipe90 확장 〉 아래에 있는 PipeA_Bend900 선택 〉 오른쪽 Inspector 〉 맨 아래 Add Component click 〉 Physics 〉 Mesh Collider 선택한다. 이제는 Pipe와 충돌을 일으키며 Pipe 속안으로도 들어갈 수 있다.

투명 분홍색 Pipe를 만들기 위해서, 왼쪽 Project 〉 아래 Create button click 〉 Material 선택한다 〉 New Material 추가된다 〉 이름을 Pipe라고 수정한다 〉 Pipe 선택 〉 오른쪽 Inspector 〉 Rendering Mode = Opaque를 Transparent로 수정, Albedo 옆의 흰색 click 〉 R = 255, G = 0, B = 255, A = 0 선택, Metalic = 0.3, Smoothness = 0.5 선택한다 〉 지금 만든 Pipe Material을 click & drag 형태로 Pipe에 입힌다.

39. Particle 사용하는 법

Asset Store tab click 〉 검색창에 particle 쓰고 〉 그 아래 FREE ONLY 선택한다. 나는 3D Games Effects Pack Free (by Creepy-cat) 다운 받음 〉 새 창이 나타나면 오른쪽 아래 Import button click 한다 〉

다운이 완료되면, 왼쪽 Project 〉 Assets 〉 Creepy Cat 〉 3D Games Effects Pack Free 〉 Prefabs 〉 아래에 particle effect들이 있다 〉 click & drag 형태로 넣으면 된다.

참고로, Google에서 "Unity Script"로 검색하면, Unity - Scripting API 나타나는데 https://docs.unity3d.com/ScriptReference/ 주소이다. 여기서 각 명령어의 의미를 찾아본다.

40. Camera 사용하는 법

Player인 ball을 따라다니는 Camera 사용법은 Camera Controller 스크립트를 통해 알아본다.

〈Script #16〉

```
// C a m e r a   C o n t r o l l e r
using UnityEngine;
using System.Collections;
using System.Collections.Generic;

public class CameraController : MonoBehaviour {
    public GameObject Player;  //2  ball
    private Vector3 offset;
              //2  distance from camera to the ball (= Player)

    // Use this for initialization
    void Start () {
```

```
        offset = transform.position - Player.transform.position;
                //2  distance from camera to the ball (= Player)
    }

    // Update is called once per frame
    void FixedUpdate ()  //2  FixedUpdate() instead of Update()
    {
        transform.position = Player.transform.position + offset;
                //2  update position of camera at every frame
    }
}
```

41. Ghost 사용하는 법

Player인 ball을 따라다니는 Ghost 사용법은 Ghost Controller 스크립트를 통해 알아본다.

```
<Script #17>
// G h o s t
using UnityEngine;
using System.Collections;

public class Ghost : MonoBehaviour {
    public Transform target;
                //8  target is the ball player that ghost will follow
    public float speed = 0.05f;  //8  moving speed of the ghost
```

```
    private bool held_X;  //11  input key 'X' to destroy Ghost
    // Use this for initialization
    void Start () {

    }

    // Update is called once per frame
    void FixedUpdate () {  //8 FixedUpdate() instead of Update()
        if (transform.position != target.position) {
              //8  if the position of ghost is not same to that of
              //the ball player
             transform.position = Vector3.MoveTowards(
              transform.position, target.position, speed);
        }

     //11  Press 'X' to destroy Ghost
        held_X = Input.GetKey(KeyCode.X);
        if (held_X == true) Destroy(gameObject);
              //11  if 'X' key is pressed, destroy Ghost
    }
}
```

42. 회전하는 Rotator 사용하는 법

제자리에서 회전하면서 item 역할을 하는 rotator 사용법은 Rotator Controller 스크립트를 통해 알아본다.

〈Script #18〉

```
// R o t a t o r
using UnityEngine;
using System.Collections;
using System.Collections.Generic;
public class Rotator : MonoBehaviour {
    // Use this for initialization
    void Start () {
    }

    // Update is called once per frame
    void FixedUpdate () {  //3 FixedUpdate() instead of Update()
        transform.Rotate(new Vector3(15, 30, 45) *
            Time.deltaTime);
            //3  update rotation of PickUp item at every frame
    }
}
```

43. 움직이는 Player 조정하는 법

Ball을 의미하는 player를 조정하는 최종적인 방법은 아래 Player Controller 스크립트를 통해 알아본다.

〈Script #19〉

```
// P l a y e r   C o n t r o l l e r
using System.Collections;
```

```
using System.Collections.Generic;
using UnityEngine;
using UnityEngine.UI;          //5  Header file for text on screen

public class PlayerController : MonoBehaviour {
    const int UP = 1;                  //13  UP direction
    const int DOWN = -1;               //13  DOWN direction

    public float speed = 10.0f;        //1  moving speed of ball

    public Text CountText;   //5  text on screen to show score
    public Text GameOverText;
            //6  text on screen to show "Game Over" message
    public Text TimerText;   //7  text on screen to show timer

    public AudioSource TickSound;   //9  wave file to make
                    // sound when player hits a pickup item

    public GameObject AutoLift_1;
                    //12  Auto Lift #1 at the right front corner
    public GameObject RangeLift_1;
            //13  Range Lift #1 at the right middle corner
    public GameObject KeyLift_1;
            //14  Key Lift #1 at the middle front corner
    public GameObject JumpPad_1;   //15  Jump Pad #1
```

```
private Rigidbody rb;              //1  ball itself
private float MoveHorizontal;
                          //1  horizontal movement of ball
private float MoveVertical;
                          //1  vertical movement of ball
private Vector3 movement;      //1  final movement of ball

private int count;         //5  number of pickup items that
                          //      the ball has collected

private int NumberOfPickUps = 12;
                                //6  number of pickup items
private float StartTime;                  //7  starting time
private bool GameHasFinished = false;
                    //7  condition if game has finished or not
private float ElapsedTime;
          //7  elapsed time = current time - start time
private string Minutes;                   //7  minutes
private string Seconds;                   //7  seconds

private bool held_Q = false;     //10  input key 'Q' to make
                                //       ball stop
private int AutoLift_1_Direction = DOWN;
          //12  initial direction of AutoLift_1 is down,
          //       where 1 = up and -1 = down
```

```
private float AutoLift_1_BottomLimit = -0.4f;
        //12  bottom limit of movement of AutoLift_1
private float AutoLift_1_TopLimit = 0.5f;
        //12  top limit of movement of AutoLift_1

private int RangeLift_1_Direction = DOWN;
        //13  initial direction of RangeLift_1 is down,
        //     where 1 = up and -1 = down
private float RangeLift_1_BottomLimit = -0.4f;
        //13  bottom limit of movement of RangeLift_1
private float RangeLift_1_TopLimit = 0.5f;
        //13  top limit of movement of RangeLift_1
private float RangeLift_1_Collision_radius = 1.3f;
        //13  collision radius of RangeLift_1,
        //     where 1.3 = 0.5 (for ball radius) +
        //     0.707 (for cube diagonal radius)
private float distance_of_RangeLift_1;
        //13  distance between the ball player
        //     and RangeLift_1
private float distance_X_of_RangeLift_1;
        //13  distance in X direction between the ball
        //     player and RangeLift_1
private float distance_Z_of_RangeLift_1;
        //13  distance in Z direction between the ball
        //     player and RangeLift_1
```

```
private float KeyLift_1_BottomLimit = -0.4f;
        //14  bottom limit of movement of KeyLift_1
private float KeyLift_1_TopLimit = 0.5f;
        //14  top limit of movement of KeyLift_1
private float KeyLift_1_Collision_radius = 1.3f;
        //14  collision radius of KeyLift_1,
        //      where 1.3 = 0.5 (for ball radius) +
        //      0.707 (for cube diagonal radius)

private float distance_of_KeyLift_1;
  //14  distance between the ball player and KeyLift_1
private float distance_X_of_KeyLift_1;
  //14  distance in X direction between the ball player
  //      and KeyLift_1
private float distance_Z_of_KeyLift_1;
  //14  distance in Z direction between the ball player
  //      and KeyLift_1
private bool held_R = false;
              //14  input key 'R' to make lift go up
private bool held_F = false;
              //14  input key 'F' to make lift go down

private float JumpPad_1_Collision_radius = 0.5f;
              //15  collision radius of JumpPad_1
private float distance_of_JumpPad_1;
```

```
  //15  distance between the ball player and JumpPad_1
private float distance_X_of_JumpPad_1;
  //15  distance in X direction between the ball player
  //      and JumpPad_1
private float distance_Z_of_JumpPad_1;
  //15  distance in Z direction between the ball player
  //      and JumpPad_1

//9  Make a wave file ready to play
void Awake() {  //9  Make a wave file ready to play

    if (TickSound == null) {      //9  if TickSound file is not
                                  //      ready to play,
        TickSound = GameObject.Find("TickSound").
                        GetComponent<AudioSource>();
          //9  find it in Hierarchy and make it ready to play
    }
}

// Use this for initialization
void Start () {
    rb = GetComponent<Rigidbody>();  //1  ball itself
    count = 0;  //5  initial value
    CountText.text = "Count: " + count.ToString();
                                  //5  show count on screen
```

```
    GameOverText.text = "";     //6  message "Game Over !!!"

    StartTime = Time.time;              //7  starting time
    TimerText.color = Color.yellow;
                         //7  set timer color to yellow
}

// Update is called once per frame
void FixedUpdate() {  //1 FixedUpdate() instead of Update()

    // Get key inputs to make ball roll around
    MoveHorizontal = Input.GetAxis("Horizontal");
                         //1  horizontal movement of ball
    MoveVertical = Input.GetAxis("Vertical");
                         //1  vertical movement of ball

    movement = new Vector3(MoveHorizontal, 0.0f,
                MoveVertical);  //1  final movement of ball
    rb.AddForce(movement * speed);
                //1  modify direction of ball movement

    if (GameHasFinished == false) {   //7  while ball is
                         // collecting 12 pickup items,
        ElapsedTime = Time.time - StartTime;
         //7  elapsed time = current time - start time
```

```
            Minutes = ((int)ElapsedTime / 60).ToString();
            Seconds = (ElapsedTime % 60).ToString("f0");
            TimerText.text = "Elapsed Time: " + Minutes + "M "
                            + Seconds + "S";
                            //7  show elapsed time on screen
        }

        //10 Press 'Q' key to make the ball player stop
        held_Q = Input.GetKey(KeyCode.Q);
        if (held_Q == true) rb.velocity = Vector3.zero;
                    //10  If 'Q key pressed, make the ball stop

        //  12, 13, 14, 15       C A L L    M A T I N E E
        UF_MATINEE();  // call for all lifts and jump pad
    }

    //4 When collision happens with other, it is called
    void OnTriggerEnter(Collider Other) {
      //4  When ball hits something, this function is called

        //4  If ball player hits something with tag = "PickUp",
        if (Other.gameObject.CompareTag("PickUp")) {
            Other.gameObject.SetActive(false);         //4  hide it

            count = count + 1;  //5  increase count by 1
```

```
        CountText.text = "Count: " + count.ToString();
                                  //5  update count on screen

        TickSound.Play();  //9  play TickSound file when
                          //  ball player hits a pickup item
    }

    if (count == NumberOfPickUps) {
         //6  If ball player has collected 12 pickup items,
        GameOverText.text = "GAME OVER";
                //6  set GameOverText = "Game Over !!!"

        GameHasFinished = true;    //7  Game has finished
         //because the ball has collected 12 pickup items
        TimerText.color = Color.red;
                          //7  change timer color to red
    }
}

//  12, 13, 14, 15        M A T I N E E
void UF_MATINEE() {

    //12  AutoLift_1 - automatic lift moving up and down
    //    in the range of [AutoLift_1_BottomLimit ..
    //    AutoLift_1_TopLimit]
```

```
if ((AutoLift_1_Direction == UP) &&
    (AutoLift_1.transform.position.y <
        AutoLift_1_TopLimit))
        AutoLift_1.transform.position =
            AutoLift_1.transform.position +
            new Vector3(0.0f, 0.01f, 0.0f);

if ((AutoLift_1_Direction == UP) &&
    (AutoLift_1.transform.position.y >=
        AutoLift_1_TopLimit))
         AutoLift_1_Direction = -1 *
            AutoLift_1_Direction;

if ((AutoLift_1_Direction == DOWN) &&
    (AutoLift_1.transform.position.y >
        AutoLift_1_BottomLimit))
        AutoLift_1.transform.position =
            AutoLift_1.transform.position +
            new Vector3(0.0f, -0.01f, 0.0f);

if ((AutoLift_1_Direction == DOWN) &&
    (AutoLift_1.transform.position.y <=
        AutoLift_1_BottomLimit))
        AutoLift_1_Direction = -1 *
            AutoLift_1_Direction;
```

```
//13 RangeLift_1 - range lift moving up and down in
//    the range of [RangeLift_1_BottomLimit ..
//    RangeLift_1_TopLimit]
// when ball player is near the range lift
distance_X_of_RangeLift_1 = rb.transform.position.x -
    RangeLift_1.transform.position.x;
                                  //13  distance in X direction
distance_Z_of_RangeLift_1 = rb.transform.position.z -
    RangeLift_1.transform.position.z;
                                  //13  distance in Z direction

distance_of_RangeLift_1 =
    Mathf.Sqrt((distance_X_of_RangeLift_1 *
    distance_X_of_RangeLift_1) +
    (distance_Z_of_RangeLift_1 *
    distance_Z_of_RangeLift_1));  //  13  distance

if (distance_of_RangeLift_1 <=
    RangeLift_1_Collision_radius)
    //13  if ball player is in the collision radius,
{
   if ((RangeLift_1_Direction == UP) &&
         (RangeLift_1.transform.position.y <
         RangeLift_1_TopLimit))
         RangeLift_1.transform.position =
```

```
                    RangeLift_1.transform.position +
                            new Vector3(0.0f, 0.01f, 0.0f);

      if ((RangeLift_1_Direction == UP) &&
              (RangeLift_1.transform.position.y >=
                    RangeLift_1_TopLimit))
                    RangeLift_1_Direction = -1 *
                            RangeLift_1_Direction;

      if ((RangeLift_1_Direction == DOWN) &&
              (RangeLift_1.transform.position.y >
                    RangeLift_1_BottomLimit))
                    RangeLift_1.transform.position =
                    RangeLift_1.transform.position +
                    new Vector3(0.0f, -0.01f, 0.0f);

      if ((RangeLift_1_Direction == DOWN) &&
              (RangeLift_1.transform.position.y <=
                    RangeLift_1_BottomLimit))
                    RangeLift_1_Direction = -1 *
                            RangeLift_1_Direction;
}

//14 KeyLift_1 - key lift moving up and down in the
//    range of [RangeLift_1_BottomLimit ..
```

```
//     RangeLift_1_TopLimit]
//      when ball player is near the range lift  and also
//     'R' or 'F' key is pressed
distance_X_of_KeyLift_1 = rb.transform.position.x -
       KeyLift_1.transform.position.x;
                               //14  distance in X direction
distance_Z_of_KeyLift_1 = rb.transform.position.z -
       KeyLift_1.transform.position.z;
                               //14  distance in Z direction


distance_of_KeyLift_1 =
       Mathf.Sqrt((distance_X_of_KeyLift_1 *
             distance_X_of_KeyLift_1) +
             (distance_Z_of_KeyLift_1 *
             distance_Z_of_KeyLift_1)); //  14  distance


if (distance_of_KeyLift_1 <= KeyLift_1_Collision_radius)
       //14  if ball player is in the collision radius,
{
      held_R = Input.GetKey(KeyCode.R);
                        //14  check if 'R' key is pressed
      held_F = Input.GetKey(KeyCode.F);
                        //14  check if 'F' key is pressed
      if ((held_R == true) &&
       (KeyLift_1.transform.position.y <
```

```
            KeyLift_1_TopLimit))
            KeyLift_1.transform.position =
                  KeyLift_1.transform.position +
                        new Vector3(0.0f, 0.01f, 0.0f);

      if ((held_F == true) &&
       (KeyLift_1.transform.position.y >
            KeyLift_1_BottomLimit))
            KeyLift_1.transform.position =
                  KeyLift_1.transform.position +
                  new Vector3(0.0f, -0.01f, 0.0f);
}

//15 JumpPad_1 - Jump Pad to make ball player fly
//    when ball player is on the Jump pad
distance_X_of_JumpPad_1 = rb.transform.position.x -
      JumpPad_1.transform.position.x;
                        //15  distance in X direction
distance_Z_of_JumpPad_1 = rb.transform.position.z -
      JumpPad_1.transform.position.z;
                        //15  distance in Z direction
distance_of_JumpPad_1 = Mathf.Sqrt(
      (distance_X_of_JumpPad_1 *
      distance_X_of_JumpPad_1) +
      (distance_Z_of_JumpPad_1 *
```

```
            distance_Z_of_JumpPad_1));              //15  distance

        if (distance_of_JumpPad_1 <=
            JumpPad_1_Collision_radius)
                //15  if ball player is on the Jump pad,
        {
            rb.AddForce(new Vector3(0.0f, 20.0f, 0.0f));
        }
    }
}
```